INDIA BOOKVARSITY
LOTUS CHOICES
Editor: Mahendra Kulasrestha

THE DHAMMAPADA

THE BOOK OF ETHICS

'He who lives in the way that has so well been taught in the Dhammapada, and is restrained, attentive, cultivating blameless works, him they call one living in the way.'

—Lord Buddha
in *Sutta Nipata*

THE GITA OF
BUDDHISM

4263/3 Ansari Road,
Darya Ganj, New Delhi- 110 002

THE DHAMMAPADA

The second book of
Khuddaka Nikaya,
Translated by
F. Max Muller

Source: The Dhammapada,
Translated by F. Max Muller,
Sacred Books of the East,
Vol. 10, Oxford University
Press, 1894.

The Dhammapada

First Edition - 2011

ISBN - 978-81-8382-237-4 (H/B)

Published by: **Lotus Press**, New Delhi

Printed at: **Anand sons**, Delhi

Buddhism, the Marvellous

– Vivekananda

Buddhism is historically the most important religion because it was the most tremendous movement the world ever saw, the most gigantic spiritual wave ever to burst upon human society. **There is no civilisation on which its effect has not been felt in some way or the other.**

The followers of Buddha were most enthusiastic and very missionary in spirit. They were the first not to remain content with the limited sphere of their mother church. They travelled east and west, north and south. They went into Persia, Asia Minor, Russia, Poland,...China, Korea, Japan,.. Burma, Siam and beyond.

The civilisation of India has died and revived several times. This is its peculiarity. At the time Buddha was born, India was in need of a great spiritual leader. There was a most powerful body of priests... The Brahmins began to arrogate powers and privileges to themselves. If a Brahmin killed a man, he would not be punished, even the most

wicked Brahmin must be worshipped....two thousand ceremonies they had invented. India was full of it in Buddha's day.

At last one man could bear it no more. He had the brain, the power and the heart—a heart as infinite as the broad sky. He learnt why men suffer, and he found the way out of suffering. **Buddha was the first great preacher of equality.** Every man and woman had the same right to attain spirituality, he opened the door of Nirvana to one and all, even the lowest were entitled to highest attainment. His teaching was bold even for India.

The religion of Buddha spread fast. It was because of the marvellous love which, for the first time in the history of humanity, devoted itself to the service not only of all men but of all living things.

Buddha's idea is that **there is no God, only man himself.** He repudiated the mentality which underlies the prevalent ideas of God. He found it made men weak and superstitious. Everything independent is happy, everything dependent is miserable.

All my life I've been very fond of Buddha. I've more veneration for that character than for any other – that boldness, that fearlessness, and that tremendous love! He was born for the good of men. He sought truth because people were in misery – how to help them, was his only concern.

And consider his marvellous brain! Believe not because an old manuscript says so, but think for yourself, search truth for yourself, realise it yourself — then if you find it beneficial, give it to people.

And consider his death. He ate food offered to him by an outcast, a *chandal*. He told his disciples not to eat this food; 'but I cannot refuse it; go to the man and tell him he has done me one of the greatest services of my life; he has released me from this body.'

His method of work and organisation was quite striking. The idea that we have today of the Church is his creation. He organised the monks and made them into a body. Even the voting by ballot is there, 560 years before Christ. **It was the foundation of Christian religion**; the Catholic Church came from Buddhism.

He was the only man who was even ready to give up his life for animals to stop a sacrifice. He once said to a king: 'If the sacrifice of a lamb helps you to go to heaven, sacrificing a man will help you better. So sacrifice me.' This man set in motion the highest moral ideas any people can have.

To many the path becomes easier if they believe in God. But the life of Buddha shows that even a man who does not believe in God, has no metaphysics, belongs to no sect and goes not to any church, or temple, and is a confessed materialist, even he can attain to the highest.

Bless You!

Editorspeak

The Gita of Buddhism

There are many religions in the world, a few of which have just one book which serves the purpose of scripture as well as ethical guidance and inspiration. On the other hand, there are many which have many books, even in hundreds—such as Hinduism, Jainism and Buddhism—in which case, they develop a select one of these, on their own in the historical process, as their most popular book—like the Bhagavadgita of Hindiusm. It is a strangely effective, and dramatic in the extreme—watching the cosmic (Vishvarupa) form of the Lord—presentation, which enhances its appeal to the common man thousandfold, giving it an upper hand over all other religious books. Buddhism has one such book, the Dhammapada, which may stand in comparison, to some extent, to it.

Buddhism from day one has been a very well planned and organised religion, which helped it

to spread, when the time came, during Asoka's reign and owing to his personal efforts, and take strong roots in the then known countries of the world. It should he noted that Lord Buddha's own contribution to its systematic development was remarkable; he was a specialist in framing rules and laying down behaviour patterns which, in later times, grew as unshakable traditions. The literature that developed was also well planned and organised into several main heads, sections and sub-sections, which they cheerfully called 'Baskets'—Pitakas—big and small—*maha* and *chulla*—, containing stories and poems of celestial palaces, *pretas*—spirits—, monks, nuns, and sub rules in large numbers for various kinds of sins, to be followed by the monks—Fa-hien visited India to find the original books of these rules—, discourses, philosophy, etc. This has been a phenomenon in itself, and in those ancient times, it must have been a tremendons effort spread over centuries. These were known as Tripitaka—Three Baskets—a summary survey of which may be interesting.

1. Vinaya Pitaka

1. Vibhanga

   Vol. I, beginning with Parajika, or sins involving expulsion.

   Vol. II, beginning with Pachittiya, or sins involving penance.

2. Khandhaka

   Vol. I, Mahavagga, the large section.

   Vol. II, Chullavagga, the small section.

3. Parivarapatha, an appendix and later resume (25 chapters).

2. Sutta Pitaka

1. Digha-nikaya, collection of long suttas (34 suttas).
2. Majjhima-nikaya, collection of middle suttas (152 suttas).
3. Samyutta-nikaya, collection of joined suttas.
4. Anguttara-nikaya, miscellaneous suttas, in divisions the length of which increases by one.
5. Khuddaka-nikaya, the collection of short suttas, consisting of—

1. Khuddakapatha, the small texts.
2. Dhammapada, law verses (423)
3. Udana, praise (82 suttas).
4. Itivuttaka, stories referring to sayings of Buddha.
5. Sutta-nipata, 70 suttas.
6. Vimanavattu, stories of Vimanas, celestial palaces.
7. Petavatthus, stories of Pretas, departed spirits.
8. Theragatha, stanzas of monks.
9. Therigatha, stanzas of nuns.
10. Jataka, former births (550 tales).
11. Niddesa, explanations of certain suttas by Sariputta.
12. Patisambhidamagga, the road of discrimination, and intuitive insight.
13. Apadana, legends.
14. Buddhavamsa, story of twenty-four preceding Buddhas and of Gotama.
15. Chariyapitaka, basket of conduct, Buddha's meritorious actions.

3. Abhidhamma Pitaka

1. Dhammasangani, numeration of conditions of life.
2. Vibhanga, disquisitions (18).
3. Kathavatthupakarana, book of subjects for discussion (1000 suttas).
4. Puggalapannatti or Pannatti, declaration on Puggala, or personality.
5. Dhatukatha, account of dhatus or elements.
6. Yamaka, pairs (ten divisions).
7. Patthanapakarana, book of causes.

These books were translated into Chinese, Tibetan and all those languages where the religion spread. The originals have been in Pali and, later on, many of them were done—even some new ones—in Sanskrit also. It is notable that **the first printed book of the world was a Buddhist work which was done in China, and to this religion goes the credit of spreading literacy**—because people were keen to read these books of good, compassion religions.

The 'Dhammapada is a small work of verses, which forms the second book of the fifth,

Khuddaka Nikaya, of the Sutta Pitaka. There are as many as fifteen books in this Nikaya, several of which sound quite interesting. But this particular collection, because of its direct approach and poetic presentation, became popular all over the Buddha-land, and was translated, in several versions in many of these countries. Interesting details of these are given in the Translator's note that follows. The title has been variously translated by modern scholars, expending more energy than is perhaps needed to do it. These are: Stanzas on the Teaching, Verses of Dhamma, Path of Virtue Path of the Law, etc. This in a way unde-rlines the scholars' utmost significance, and love, they have given to this sacred religious literature. I would personally prefer to translate it simply as The Book of Ethics, or The Buddha Ethics, or to be modern, Be Good, Do Your Duty; one may take what pleases him.

Like Vivekananda, I am much attracted by Buddha, and some of his basic ideas. I would be glad to see his spirit spreading in difficult modern times. For that purpose I include the present book in this series. May He Bless All!

Translatorspeak

The Most Favourite

It has been a great and unexpected pleasure to me to have to bring out the third edition of my translation of the Dhammapada. The first was published in 1870, the second in 1881. I began it in 1845 during my stay at Paris with Burnouf, who was then almost the only scholar who could read Pali texts. At that time Pali scholarship had not yet become a special and independent study, but it was a kind of annexe to Sanskrit. Some advance was made by Spiegel and Westergaard, but the real impulse to an independent and scholarlike study of Pali literature came from my friend Childers, the author of the first Pali Dictionary, published in 1875. After its publication the progress of Pali scholarship has been very rapid and the number of Pali texts and translations has increased very considerably.

The favourite text seems to have been the Dhammapada. It is certainly a most interesting

colloection of verses, giving a trustworthy picture of Buddhist thoughts, particularly in its practical and moral character. Consisting of short sentences, it seems at first an easy book to translate, but the very fact that these verses stand by themselves without any context to throw light on them, creates a pecliar difficulty, much the same as that with which the readers of another elementary book, the Hitopadesa, are well acquainted. Like the Hitopadesa, the Dhammapada also may be called an easy and at the same time a very difficult book. The meaning of the very title 'Dhammapada,' is still contested. I have produced whatever arguments I could in support of the meaning of 'Path of Virtue' or 'Path of the Law.' For titles are often fanciful, and mere scholarship is not sufficient to enable us to speak with magisterial assurance.

No one who has not himself tried to translate Oriental thought into any European language can have any idea of the almost impossible task of finding words in any of these modern languages exactly corresponding to the ancient terms of Eastern religion or philosophy. To find terms

exactly corresponding to the varied terminology of Buddhism is simply impossible. They do not exist, as little as there are moders coins corresponding exactly to a *karshapana*. Here nothing remains but to use terms of more general meaning which at all events are not wrong, and which, though they do not exactly cover the Pali terms, yet include them. This is the rule I have tried to follow throughout.

The Dhammapada forms part of the Pali Buddhist canon, though its exact place varies according to different authorities.

Those who divide that canon into three Pitakas or baskets, the Vinaya-pitaka, Sutta-pitaka, and Abhidhamma-pitaka, assign the Dhammapada to the Sutta-pitaka. That Pitaka consists of five Nikayas; the fifth, or Khuddaka-nikaya, comprehends Dhammapada.

There is a commentary on the Dhammapada in Pali, and supposed to be written by Buddhaghosa, in the first half of the fifth century A.D. In explaining the verses of the Dhammapada, the commentator gives for every or nearly every verse a parable to illustrate its meaning, which is

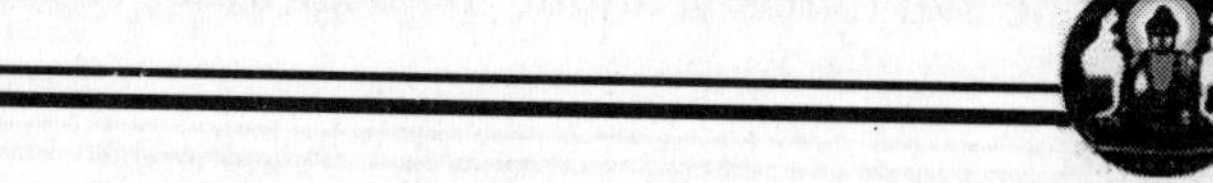

likewise believed to have been uttered by Buddha in his intercourse with his disciples, or in preaching to the multitudes that came to hear him.

In translating the verses of the Dhammapada, I have followed the edition of the Pali text, published in 1855 by Dr. Fausboll, and I have derived great advantage from his Latin translation, his notes, and his copious extracts from Buddhaghosa's commentary. I have also consulted translations, either of the whole of the Dhammapada, or of portions of it, by Burnouf, Gogerly, Upham, Weber, and others.

It was a discovery of great interest, when Mr. Beal announced that the text of the Dhammapada was not restricted to the southern Buddhists, but that similar collections existed in the north, and had been translated into Chinese. It was equally important when Schiefner proved the existence of the same work in the sacred canon of the Tibetans.

There are, as Mr. Beal informs us, four principal copies of what may be called Dhammapada in Chinese, the first dating from the Wu dynasty, about the beginning of the third

century A.D. This translation, called 'Fa-kheu-king,' is the work of a Shaman Wei-Ki-lan and others. Its title means 'The Sutra of Law Verses.'

In the preface to the 'Fa-kheu-king' we are told that the original, which consisted of 500 verses, was brought from India by Wai-Ki-lan in 223 A.D., and that it was translated into Chinese with the help of another Indian called Tsiangsin. After the translation was finished, thirteen sections were added, making up the whole to 752 verses, 14,580 words, and 39 chapters.

If the Chinese translation is compared with the Pali text, it appears that the two agree from the 9th to the 35th chapter, with the exception of the 33rd, so far as their subjects are concerned, though the Chinese has in these chapters 79 verses more than the Pali, but the Chinese translation has eight additional chapters in the beginning (On Intemperance, Inciting to Wisdom, The Sravaka, Simple Faith, Observance of Duty, Reflection, Loving Kindness, and Conversation), and four at the end (Nirvana, Birth and Death, Profit of Religion, and Good Fortune), and one between the 24th and 25th chapter of the Pali text

(Advantageous Service), all of which are absent in our Pali texts. This the most ancient Chinese translation has now been rendered into English by Mr. Beal, but he assures us that it is a faithful reproduction of the original. The book which he has chosen for translation is 'Fa-kheu-pi-u', i.e., parables connected with the Dhammapada and translated into Chinese by two Shamans of the western Tsin dynasty (A.D. 265-313).

A third Chinese version is called 'Chuh-yan-king,' i.e., the Sutra of the Dawn, consisting of seven volumes. Its author was Dhamatrata, its translator Chu-fo-nien (Buddhasmriti), about 410 A.D. The Ms. of the work is said to have been brought from India by a Shaman Sanghabha-danga, about 345 A.D. It is a much more extensive work in 33 chapters, the last being, as in the Pali text, on the Brahmins.

A fourth translation dates from the Sung dynasty (800 or 900 A.D.), and in it too, the authorship of the text is ascribed to Arya Dharmatrata.

The Tibetan translation of Dhammapada was discovered by Schiefner in the 28th volume of the

Sutras, in the collection called Udanavarga. It contains 33 chapters and more than 1000 verses, of which about one-fourth only can be traced in the Pali text. The same collection is found also in the Tanjur, Vol. 71 of the Sutras, followed by commentary, the Udanavarga-vivarana by Acharya Prajnavarman. Unfortunately, Schiefner's intention of publishing a translation of it has been frustrated by his death. All that he gives us in his last paper is the Tibetan text with translation of another shorter collection, the Gathas-angraha, by Vasubandhu, published in the 72nd volume of the Sutras in Tanjur, and accompanied by a commentary.

I cannot see any reason why we should not treat the verses of the Dhammapada, if not as the utterances of Buddha, at least as what were believed by the members of the Council under Asoka, in 242 B.C., to have been the utterances of the founder of their religion.

The idea of representing life, and particularly the life of the faithful, as a path of duty or virtue leading to deliverance, (in Sanskrit *dharamapatha*) is very familiar to Buddhists. The four great truths

of their religion consist in the recognition of the following principles: 1. that there is suffering; 2. that there is a cause of that suffering; 3. that such cause can be removed; 4. that there is a way of deliverance, the doctrine of Buddha. This way is Ashtanga-marga, the eightfold way, taught by Buddha, and leading to Nirvana. The faithful advances on the road, *padat padam*, step by step, and it is therefore called *patipada*, lit.. by step.

Oxford
1894

Contents

The Dhammapada

Buddha Meditations

Lord Buddha, Java

1

Thoughts

All that we are is the result of what we have thought: it is founded on our thoughts, it is made up of our thoughts. If a man speaks or acts with an evil thought, pain follows him, as the wheel follows the foot of the ox that draws the carriage.

All that we are is the result of what we have thought: it is founded on our thoughts, it is made up of our thoughts. If a man speaks or acts with a pure thought, happiness follows him, like a shadow that never leaves him.

'He abused me, he beat me, he defeated me, he robbed me,'—in those who harbour such thoughts hatred will never cease.

'He abused me, he beat me, he defeated me, he robbed me,'—in those who do not harbour such thoughts hatred will cease.

For hatred does not cease by hatred at any time: hatred ceases by love, this is an old rule.

The world does not know that we must all come to an end here;—but those who know it, their quarrels cease at once.

He who lives looking for pleasures only, his senses uncontrolled, immoderate in his food, idle, and weak, Mara (the tempter) will certainly overthrow him, as the wind throws down a weak tree.

He who lives without looking for pleasures, his senses well controlled, moderate in his food, faithful and strong, him Mara will certainly overthrow, any more than wind throws down a rocky mountain.

He who wishes to put on the yellow dress without having cleansed himself from sin, who disregards also temperance and truth, is unworthy of the yellow dress.

But he who has cleansed himself from sin, is well grouded in all virtues, and endowed also with temperance and truth, he is worthy of the yellow dress.

They who imagine truth in untruth, and see untruth in truth, never arrive at truth, but follow vain desires.

They who know truth in truth, and untruth in untruth, arrive at truth, and follow true desires.

As rain breaks through an ill-thatched house, passion will break through an unreflecting mind.

As rain does not break through a well-thatched house, passion will not break through a well-reflecting mind.

The evil-doer mourns in this world, and he mourns in the next; he mourns in both. He mourns and suffers when he sees the evil result of his own work.

The virtuous man delights in this world, and he delights in the next; he delights in both. He delights and rejoices, when he sees the purity of his own work.

The evil-doer suffers in this world, and he suffers in the next; he suffers in both. He suffers when he thinks of the evil he has done; he suffers more when going on the evil path.

The virtuous man is happy in this world, and he is happy in he next; he is happy in both. He is happy when he thinks of the good he has done; he is still more happy when going on the good path.

The thoughtless man, even if he can recite a large portion of the Law (Dhamma), but is not a

doer of it, has no share in the priesthood, but is like a cowherd counting the cows of others.

The follower of the Law, even if he can recite only a small portion of of the Law, but, having forsaken passion and hatred and foolishness, possesses true knowledge and serenity of mind, he, caring for nothing in this world or that to come, has indeed a share in the priesthood.

2

Earnestness

Earnestness is the path of immortality, Nirvana, thoughtlessness the path of death. Those who are in earnest do not die, those who are thoughtless are as if dead already.

Having understood this clearly, those who are advanced in earnestness delight in earnestness, and rejoice in the knowledge of the Ariyas (Aryas), the elect.

These wise people, meditative, steady, always possesserd of strong powers, attain to Nirvana, the highest happiness.

If an earnest person has roused himself, if he is not forgetful, if his deeds are pure, if he acts with consideration, if he restrains himself and lives according to Law,—then his glory will increase.

By rousing himself, by earnestness, by restraint and control, the wise man may make for himself an island which no flood can overwhelm.

Fools follow after vanity, men of evil wisdom. The wise man keeps earnestness as his best jewel.

Follow not after vanity, nor after the enjoyment of love and lust. He who is earnest and meditative, obtains ample joy.

When the learned man drives away vanity by earnestness, he, the wise, climbing the terraced heights of wisdom, looks down upon the fools; free from sorrow he looks down upon the sorrowing crowd, as one that stands on a mountain looks down upon them that stand upon the plain.

Earnest among the thoughtless, awake among the sleepers, the wise man advances like a racer, leaving behind the hack.

By earnestness did Maghavan (Indra) rise to the lordship of the gods. People praise earnestness; thoughtlessness is always blamed.

A Bhikshu who delights in earnestness, who looks with fear on thoughtlessness, moves about like fire, burning all his fetters, small or large.

A Bhikshu who delights in reflection, who looks with fear away from his perfect state—he is close upon Nirvana.

3

Balance

As a fletcher makes straight his arrow, a wise man makes straight his trembling and unsteady thought, which is difficult to guard, difficult to hold back.

As a fish taken from his watery home and thrown on the dry ground, our thoughts tremble all over in order to escape the dominion of Mara, the tempter.

It is good to tame the mind, which is difficult to hold in and flighty, rushing wherever it listeth; a tamed mind brings happiness.

Let the wise man guard his thoughts, for they are difficult to perceive, very artful, and they rush wherever they list: thoughts well guarded bring happiness.

Those who bridle their mind which travels far, moves about alone, is without a body, and hides in the chamber of the heart, will be free from the bonds of Mara, the tempter.

If a man's faith is unsteady, if he does not know the true Law, if his peese of mind is troubled, his knowledge will never be perfect.

If a man's thoughts are not dissipated, if his mind is not perplexed, if he has ceased to think of good or evil, then there is no fear for him while he is watchful.

Knowing that this body is fragile like a jar, and making his thought firm like a fortress, one should attack Mara, the tempter, with the weapon of knowledge, one should watch him when conquered, and should never rest.

Before long, alas! this body will lie on the earth, despised, without understanding, like a useless log.

Whatever a hater may do to a hater, or an enemy to any enemy, a wrongly-directed mind will do him greater mischief.

Not a mother, not a father will do so much, nor any other relatives; a well-directed mind will do us greater service.

Apsara, Sigiria, Srilanka

4

Flowers

Who shall overcome this earth, and the world of Yama, the lord of the departed, and the world of the gods? Who shall find out the plainly shown path of virtue, as a clever man finds the right flower?

The disciple will overcome the earth, and the world of Yama, and the world of the gods. The disciple will find out the plainly shown path of virtue, as a clever man finds the right flower.

He who knows that this body is like froth, and has learnt that it is as unsubstantial as a mirage, will break the flower-pointed arrow of Mara, and never see the king of death.

Death carries off a man who is gathering flowers, and whose mind is distracted, as a flood carries off a sleeping village.

Death subdues a man who is gathering flowers, and whose mind is distracted, before he is satiated in his pleasures.

As the bee collects nectar and departs without injuring the flower, or its colour or scent, so let a sage dwell in his village.

Not the perversities of others, not their sins of commission or ommission, but his own misdeeds and negligences should a sage take notice of.

Like a beautiful flower, full of colour, but without scent, are the fine but fruitless words of him who does not act accordingly.

But, like a beautiful flower, full of colour and full of scent, are the fine but fruitful words of him who acts accordingly.

As many kinds of wreaths can be made from a heap of flowers, so many good things may be achieved by a mortal when once he is born.

The scent of flowers does not travel against the wind, nor that of sandalwood, or of Tagara and Mallika flowers; but the odour of good people travels even against the wind; a good man pervades every place.

Sandalwood or Tagara, a lotus flower, or a Vassiki, among these sorts of perfumes, the perfume of virtue is unsurpassed.

Mean is the scent that comes from Tagara

and sandalwood;—the perfume of those who possess virtue rises up to the gods as the highest.

Of the people who possess these virtues, who live without thoughtlessness, and who are emancipated through true knowledge, Mara, the tempter, never finds the way.

As on a heap of rubbish cast upon the highway the lily will grow full of sweet perfume and delight, thus among those who are mere rubbish the disciple of the truly enlightened Buddha shines forth by his knowledge above the blinded worldling.

5
The Fool

Long is the night to him who is awake; long is a mile to him who is tired; long is life to the foolish who do not know the true Law.

If a traveller does not meet with one who is his better, or his equal, let him firmly keep to his solitary journey; there is no companionship with a fool.

'These sons belong to me, and this wealth belongs to me,' with such thoughts a fool is tormented. He himself does not belong to himself; how much less sons and wealth?

The fool who knows his foolishness, is wise at least so far. But a fool who thinks himself wise, he is called a fool indeed.

If a fool be associated with a wise man even all his life, he will perceive the truth as little as a spoon perceives the taste of soup.

If an intelligent man be associated for one minute only with a wise man, he will soon perceive

the truth, as the tongue perceives the taste of soup.

Fools of poor understanding have themselves for their greatest enemies, for they do evil deeds which bear bitter fruits.

That deed is not well done of which a man must repent, and the reward of which he receives crying and with a tearful face.

No, that deed is well done of which a man does not repent, and the reward of which he receives gladly and cheerfully.

As long as the evil deed done does not bear fruit, the fool thinks it is like honey; but when it ripens, then the fool suffers grief.

Let a fool month after month eat his food like an ascetic with the tip of a blade of Kusa grass, yet is he not worth the sixteenth particle of those who have well weighed the Law.

An evil deed, like newly-drawn milk, does not turn suddenly; smouldering, like fire covered by ashes, it follows the fool.

And when the evil deed, after it has become known, turns to sorrow for the fool, then it destroys his bright lot, nay, it cleaves his head.

Let the fool wish for a false reputation, for

precedence among the Bhikshus, for lordship in the convents, for worship among other people!

'May both the layman and he who has left the world think that this is done by me; may they be subject to me in everything which is to be done or is not to be done,' thus is the mind of the fool, and his desire and pride increase.

'One is the road that leads to wealth, another the road that leads to Nirvana;' if the Bhikshu, the disciple of Buddha, has learnt this, he will not yearn for honour, he will strive after separation from the world.

6
The Wise Man

If you see a man who shows you what is to be avoided, who administers reproofs, and is intelligent, follow that wise man as you would one who tells of hidden treasures; it will be better, not worse, for him who follows him.

Let him admonish, let him teach, let him forbid what is improper!—he will be beloved of the good, by the bad he will be hated.

Do not have evil-doers for friends, do not have low people for friends: have virtuous people for friends, have for friends the best of men.

He who drinks in the law lives happily with a serene mind: the sage rejoices always in the law, as preached by the elect, Ariyas.

Well-makers lead the water wherever they like; fletchers bend the arrow; carpenters bend a log of wood; wise people fashion themselves.

As a solid rock is not shaken by the wind, wise people falter not amidst blame and praise.

Wise people, after they have listened to the laws, become serene, like a deep, smooth, and still lake.

Good men indeed walk warily under all circumstances; good men speak not out of a desire for sensual gratification; whether touched by happiness or sorrow, wise people never appear elated or depressed.

If, whether for his own sake, or for the sake of others, a man wishes neither for a son, nor for wealth, nor for lordship, and if he does not wish for his own success by unfair means, then he is good, wise, and virtuous.

Few are there among men who arrive at the other shore, become Arhats; the other people here run up and down the shore.

But those who, when the Law has been well preached to them, follow the Law, will pass over the dominion of death, however difficult to cross.

A wise man should leave the dark state of ordinary life, and follow the bright state of the Bhikshu. After going from his home to a homeless state, he should in his retirement look for enjoyment where enjoyment seemed difficult.

Leaving all pleasures behind, and calling nothing his own, the wise man should purge himself from all the troubles of the mind.

Those whose mind is well grounded in the seven elements of knowledge, who without clinging to anything, rejoice in freedom from attachment, whose appetites have been conquered, and who are full of light, they are free even in this world.

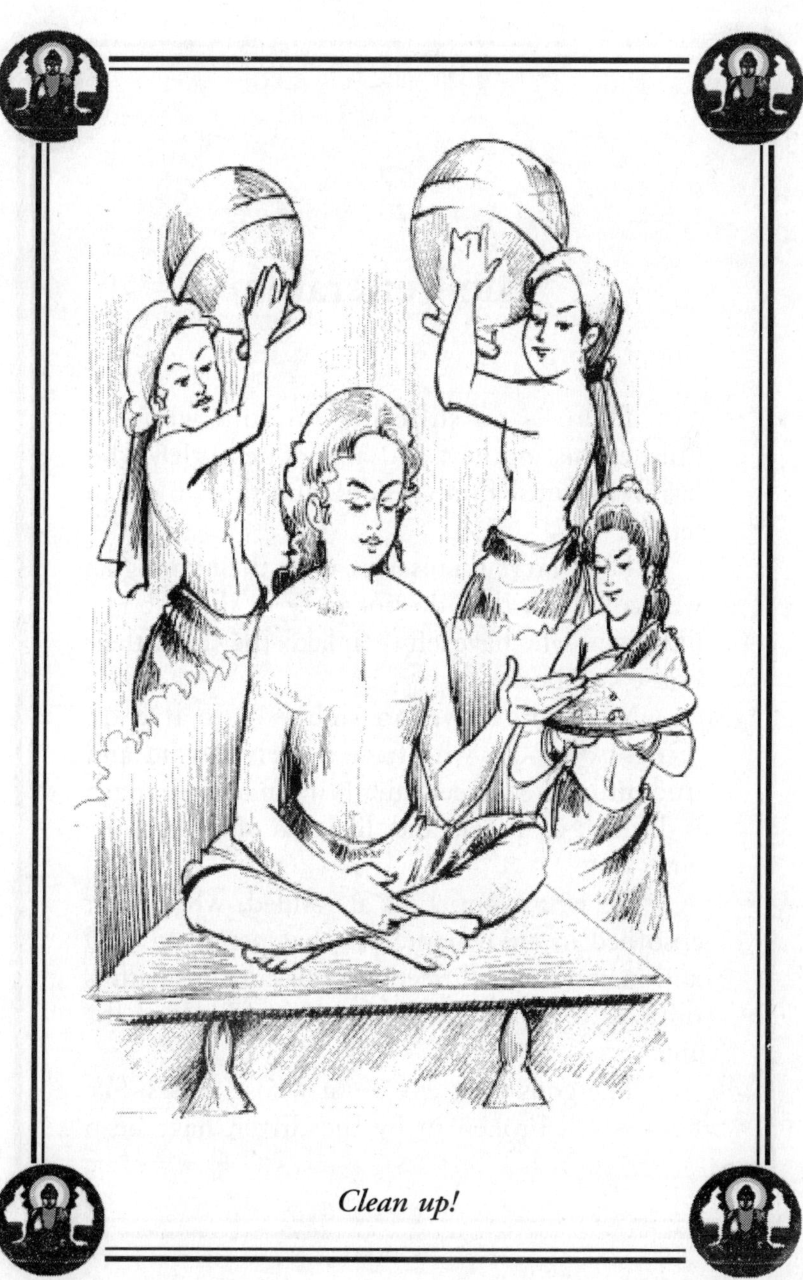

Clean up!

7

The Venerable

There is no suffering for him who has finished his journey, and abandoned grief, who has freed himself on all sides, and thrown off all fetters.

They exert themselves with their thoughts well-collected, they do not tarry in their abode; like swans who have left their lake, they leave their house and home.

Men who have no riches, who live on recognised food, who have perceived void and unconditioned freedom, Nirvana, their path is difficult to understand, like that of birds in the air.

He whose appetites are stilled, who is not absorbed in enjoyment, who has perceived void and unconditioned freedom, Nirvana, his path is difficult to understand, like that of birds in the air.

The gods even envy him whose senses, like horses well broken in by the driver, have been

subdued, who is free from pride, and free from appetites;

Such a one who does his duty is tolerant like the earth, or like a threshold; he is like a lake without mud; no new births are in store for him.

His thought is quiet, quiet are his word and deed, when he has obtained freedom by true knowledge, when he has thus become a quiet man.

The man who is free from credulity, but knows the uncreated, who has cut all ties, removed all temptations, renounced all desires, he is the greatest of men.

In a hamlet or in a forest, on sea or on dry land, wherever venerable persons, Arahant, dwell, that place is delightful.

Forests are delightful; where the world finds no delight, there the passionless will find delight, for they look not for pleasures.

8

The Thousands

Even though a speech be of a thousand words, but made up of senseless words, one word of sense is better, which if a man hears, he becomes quiet.

Even though a Gatha (poem) be of a thousand words, but made up of senseless words, one word of a Gatha is better, which if a man hears, he becomes quiet.

Though a man recite a hundred Gathas made up of senseless words, one word of the law is better, which if a man hears, he becomes quiet.

If one man conquer in battle a thousand times thousand men, and if another conquer himself, he is the greatest of conquerors.

One's own self conquered is better than all other people; not even a god, a Gandharva, not Mara with Brahman could change into defeat the victory of a man who has vanquished himself, and always lives under restraint.

If a man for a hundred year sacrifice month by month with a thousand, and if he but for one moment pay homage to a man whose soul is grounded in true knowledge, better is that homage than a sacrifice for a hundred years.

If a man for a hundred years worship Agni (fire) in the forest, and if he but for one moment pay homage to a man whose soul is grounded in true knowledge, better is that homage than sacrifice for a hundred years.

Whatever a man sacrifice in this world as an offering or as an oblation for a whole year in order to gain merit, the whole of it is not worth a quarter; reverence shown to the righteous is better.

He who always greets and constantly reveres the aged, four things will increase to him: life, beauty, happiness, power.

But he who lives a hundred years, vicious and unrestrained, a life of one day is better if a man is virtuous and reflecting.

And he who lives a hundred years, ignorant and unrestrained, a life of one day is better if a man is wise and reflecting.

And he who lives a hundred years, idle and

unrestrained, a life of one day is better if a man has attained firm strength.

And he who lives a hundred years, not seeing beginning and end, a life of one day is better if a man sees beginning and end.

And he who lives a hundred years, not seeing the immortal place, a life of one day is better if a man sees the immortal place.

And he who lives a hundred years, not seeing the highest Law, a life of one day is better if a man sees the highest Law.

9

Evil

A man should hasten towards the good, and should keep his thought away from evil; if a man does what is good slothfully, his mind delights in evil.

If a man commits a sin, let him not do it again; let him not delight in sin; the accumulation of evil is painful.

If a man does what is good, let him do it again; let him delight in it; the accumulation of good is delightful.

Even an evil-doer sees happiness so long as his evil deed does not ripen; but when his evil deed ripens, then does the evil-doer see evil.

Even a good man sees evil days so long as his good deed does not ripen; but when his good deed ripens, then does the good man see good things.

Let no man think lightly of evil, saying in his heart: It will not come nigh unto me. Even by

the falling of water-drops a water-pot is filled; the fool becomes full of evil, even if he gather it little by little.

Let no man think lightly of good, saying in his heart: It will not come nigh unto me. Even by the falling of water-drops a water-pot is filled; the wise man becomes full of good, even if he gather it little by little.

Let a man avoid evil deeds, as a merchant, if he has few companions and carries much wealth, avoids a dangerous road; as a man who loves life avoids poison.

He who has no wound on his hand, may touch poison with his hand; poison does not affect one who has no wound; nor is there evil for one who does not commit evil.

If a man offend a harmless, pure, and innocent person, the evil falls back upon that fool, like light dust thrown up against the wind.

Some people are born again; evil-doers go to hell; righteous people go to heaven; those who are free from all worldly desires attain Nirvana.

Not in the sky, not in the midst of the sea, not if we enter into the clefts of the mountains, is

there known a spot in the whole world where a man might be freed from an evil deed.

Not in the sky, not in the midst of the sea, not if we enter into the clefts of the mountains, is there known a spot in the whole world where death could not overcome the mortal.

10

Punishment

All men tremble at punishment, all men fear death; remember that you are like unto them, and do not kill, nor cause slaughter.

All men tremble at punishment, all men love life; remember that thou are like unto them, and do not kill, nor cause slaughter.

He who, seeking his own happiness, punishes or kills beings who also long for happiness, will not find happiness after death.

He who, seeking his own happiness, does not punish or kill beings who also long for happiness, will find happiness after death.

Do not speak harshly to anybody; those who are spoken to, will answer thee in the same way. Angry speech is painful, blows for blows will touch thee.

If, like a shattered metal plate (gong), thou utter nothing, then thou hast reached Nirvana; anger is not known to thee.

As a cowherd with his staff drives his cows into the stable, so do Age and Death drive the life of men.

A fool does not know when he commits his evil deeds; but the wicked man burns by his own deeds, as if burnt by fire.

He who inflicts pain on innocent and harmless persons, will soon come to one of these ten states:

He will have cruel suffering, loss, injury of the body, heavy affliction, or loss of mind.

Or a misfortune coming from the king, or a fearful accusation. or loss of relations, or destruction of treasures,

Or lightning-fire will burn his houses; and when his body is destroyed, the fool will go to hell.

Not nakedness, not plaited hair, not dirt, not fasting, or lying on the earth, not rubbing with dust, not sitting motionless, can purify a mortal who has not overcome desires.

He who, though dressed in fine apparel, exercises tranquillity, is quiet, subdued, restrained, chaste, and has ceased to find fault with all other

beings, he indeed is a brahmin, an ascetic, sramana, a friar, bhikshu.

Is there in this world any man so restrained by shame that he does not provoke reproof, as a noble horse the whip?

Like a noble horse when touched by the whip, be ye strenuous and eager, and by faith, by virtue, by energy, by meditation, by discernment of the law, you will overcome this great pain, perfect in knowledge and in behaviour, and never forgetful.

Well-makers lead the water wherever they like; fletchers bend the arrow; carpenters bend a log of wood; good people fashion themselves.

Seek a light !

11

Old Age

How is there laughter, how is there joy, as this world is always burning? Do you not seek a light, ye who are surrounded by darkness?

Look at this dressed-up lump, covered with wounds, joined together, sickly, full of many schemes, but which has no strength, no hold!

This body is wasted, full of sickness, and frail; this heap of corruption breaks to pieces, life indeed ends in death.

After one has looked at those grey bones, thrown away like gourds in the autumn, what pleasure is there left in life!

After a stronghold has been made of the bones, it is covered with flesh and blood, and there dwell in it old age and death, pride and deceit.

The brilliant chariots of kings are destroyed, the body also approaches destruction, but the virtue of good people never approaches destruction,—thus do the good say to the good.

A man who has learnt little, grows old like an ox; his flesh grows, but his knowledge does not grow.

Looking for the maker of this tabernacle, I have run through a course of many births, not finding him; and painful is birth again and again. But now, maker of the tabernacle, thou hast been seen; thou shalt not make up this tabernacle again. All thy rafters are broken, thy ridge-pole is sundered; the mind, approaching the Eternal (Nirvana), has attained to the extinction of all desires.

Men who have not observed proper discipline, and have not gained wealth in their youth, perish like old herons in a lake without fish.

Men who have not observed proper discipline, and have not gained wealth in their youth, lie like broken bows, sighing after the past.

12
Self

If a man hold himself dear, let him watch himself carefully; during one at least out of the three watches a wise man should be watchful.

Let each man direct himself first to what is proper, then let him teach others; thus a wise man will not suffer.

If a man make himself as he teaches others to be, then, being himself well subdued, he may subdue others; for one's own self is difficult to subdue.

Self is the lord of self, who else could be the lord? With self well subdued, a man finds a lord such as few can find.

The evil done by oneself, self-begotten, self-bred, crushes the foolish, as a diamond breaks even a precious stone.

He whose wickedness is very great, brings himself down to that state where his enemy wishes him to be, as a creeper does with the tree which it surrounds.

Bad deeds, and deeds hurtful to ourselves, are easy to do; what is beneficial and good, that is very difficult to do.

The foolish man who scorns the rule of the venerable, Arahat, of the elect, Ariya, of the virtuous, and follows a false doctrine, he bears fruit to his own destruction, like the fruits of the Katthaka reed.

By oneself the evil is done, by oneself one suffers; by oneself evil is left undone, by oneself one is purified. The pure and the impure stand and fall by themselves, no one can purify another.

Let no one forget his own duty for the sake of another's, however great; let a man, after he has discerned his own duty, be always attentive to his duty.

13
The World

Do not follow the evil law! Do not live on in thoughtlessness! Do not follow false doctrine! Be not a friend of the world.

Rouse thyself! Do not be idle! Follow the law of virtue! The virtuous rests in bliss in this world and in the next.

Follow the law of virtue; do not follow that of sin. The virtuous rests in bliss in the world and in the next.

Look upon the world as you would on a bubble, look upon it as you would on a mirage: the king of death does not see him who thus looks down upon the world.

Come, look at this world, glittering like a royal chariot; the foolish are immersed in it, but the wise do not touch it.

He who formerly was reckless and afterwards became sober, brightens up this world, like the moon when freed from clouds.

He whose evil deeds are covered by good deeds, brightens up this world, like the moon when freed from clouds.

This world is dark, few only can see here; a few only go to heaven, like birds escaped from the net.

The swans go on the path of the sun, they go miraculously through the ether; the wise are led out of this world, when they have conquered Mara and his train.

If a man has transgressed the one law, and speaks lies, and scoffs at another world, there is no evil he will not do.

The uncharitable do not go to the world of the gods; fools only do not praise liberality; a wise man rejoices in liberality, and through it becomes blessed in the other world.

Better than sovereignty over the earth, better than going to heaven, better than lordship over all worlds, is the reward of Sotapatti, the first step one takes in holiness.

14

The Awakened

He whose conquest cannot be conquered again, into whose conquest no one in this world enters, by what track can you lead him, the Awakened, the Omniscient, the trackless?

He whom no desire with its snares and poisons can lead astray, by what track can you lead him, the Awakened, the Omniscient, the trackless?

Even the gods envy those who are awakened and not forgetful, who are given to meditation, who are wise, and who delight in the repose of retirement from the world.

Difficult to obtain is the conception of men, difficult is the life of mortals, difficult is the hearing of the True Law, difficult is the birth of the Awakened, the attainment of Buddhahood.

Not to commit any sin, to do good, and to purify one's mind, that is the teaching of all the Awakened.

The Awakened call patience the highest penance, long-suffereing the highest Nirvana; for he is not an anchorite, pravrajita, who strikes others, he is not an ascetic, sramana, who insults others.

Not to blame, not to strike, to live restrained under the Law, to be moderate in eating, to sleep and sit alone, and to dwell on the highest thoughts,—this is the teaching of the Awakened.

There is no satisfying lusts, even by a shower of gold pieces; he who knows that lusts have a short taste and cause pain, he is wise;

Even in heavenly pleasures he finds no satisfaction, the disciple who is fully awakened, delights only in the destruction of all desires.

Men, driven by fear, go to many a refuge, to mountains and forests, to groves and sacred trees.

But that is not a safe refuge, that is not the best refuge; a man is not delivered from all pains after having gone to that refuge.

He who takes refuge with Buddha, the Dhamma, and the Sangh; he who, with clear understanding, sees the four holy truths:

Pain, the origin of pain, the destruction of pain, and the eightfold holy way that leads to the quieting of pain;—

That is the safe refuge, that is the best refuge; having gone to that refuge, a man is delivered from all pain.

A supernatural person, a Buddha, is not easily found, he is not born everywhere. Wherever such a sage is born, that race prospers.

Happy is the arising of the awakened, happy is the teaching of the True Law, happy is peace in the Sangh, happy is the devotion of those who are at peace.

He who pays homage to those who deserve homage, whether the awakened Buddha or their disciples, those who have overcome the host of evils, and crossed the flood of sorrow, he who pays homage to such as have found deliverance and know no fear, his merit can never be measured by anybody.

15

Happiness

We live happily indeed, not hating those who hate us! among men who hate us we dwell free from hatred!

We live happily indeed, free from ailments among the ailing! among men who are ailing let us dwell free from ailments!

We live happily indeed, free from greed among the greedy! among men who are greedy let us dwell free from greed!

We live happily indeed, though we call nothing our own! We shall be like the bright gods, feeding on happiness.

Victory breeds hatred, for the conquered is unhappy. He who has given up both victory and defeat, he, the contented, is happy.

There is no fire like passion; there is no losing throw like hatred; there is no pain like this body; there is no happiness higher than rest.

Hunger is the worst of diseases, the elements of the body the greatest evil; if one knows this truly, that is Nirvana, the highest happiness.

Health is the greatest of gifts, contentedness the best of riches; trust is the best of relationships, Nirvana the highest happiness.

He who has tasted the sweetness of solitude and tranquillity, is free from fear and free from sin, while he tastes the sweetness of drinking in the Law.

The sight of the elect, Ariya, is good, to live with them is always happiness; if a man does not see fools, he will be truly happy.

He who walks in the company of fools, suffers a long way; company with fools, as with an enemy, is always painful; company with the wise is pleasure, like meeting with kinsfolk.

Therefore, one ought to follow the wise, the intelligent, the learned, the much enduring, the dutiful, the elect; one ought to follow such good and wise men, as the moon follows the path of the stars.

What is good ?

16

Pleasure

He who gives himsefl to vanity, and does not give himself to meditation, forgeting the real aim of life and grasping at pleasure, will in time envy him who has exerted himself in meditation.

Let no man ever cling to what is pleasant, or to what is unpleasant. Not to see what is pleasant is pain, and it is pain to see what is unpleasant.

Let, therefore, no man love anything; loss of the beloved is evil. Those who love nothing, and hate nothing, have no fetters.

From pleasure comes grief, from pleasure comes fear; he who is free from pleasure, knows neither grief nor fear.

From affection comes grief, from affection comes fear; he who is free from affection, knows neither grief nor fear.

From lust comes grief, from lust comes fear; he who is free from lust, knows neither grief nor fear.

From love comes grief, from love comes fear; he who is free from love, knows neither grief nor fear.

From greed comes grief, from greed comes fear; he who is free from greed, knows neither grief nor fear.

He who possesses virtue and intelligence, who is just, speaks the truth, and does what is his own business, him the world will hold dear.

He in whom a desire for the Ineffable, Nirvana, has sprung up, who in his mind is satisfied, and whose thoughts are not bewildered by love, he is called Urdhvamsrotas, carried upwards by the stream.

Kinsmen, friends, and lovers salute a man who has been long away, and returns safe from afar.

In like manner his good works receive him who has done good, and has gone from this world to the other;—as kinsmen receive a friend on his return.

17

Anger

Let a man leave anger, let him forsake pride, let him overcome all bondage! No sufferings befall the man who is not attached to name and form, and who calls nothing his own.

He who holds back rising anger like a rolling chariot, him I call a real driver; other people are but holding the reins.

Let a man overcome anger by love, let him overcome evil by good; let him overcome the greedy by liberality, the liar by truth!

Speak the truth, do not yield to anger; give, if thou art asked for some; by these three steps thou wilt go near the gods.

The sages who injure nobody, and who always control their body, they will go to the unchangeable place, Nirvana, where, if they have gone, they will suffer no more.

Those who are ever watchful, who study day and night, and who strive after Nirvana, their passions will come to an end.

This is an old saying, O Atula, this is not as if of to-day: 'They blame him who sits silent, they blame him who speaks much, they also blame him who says little; there is no one on earth who is not blamed.'

There never was, there never will be, nor is there now, a man who is always blamed, or a man who is always praised.

But he whom those who discriminate, praise continually day after day, as without blemish, wise, rich in knowledge and virtue, who would dare to blame him, like a coin made of gold from the Jambu river? Even the gods praise him, he is preaised even by Brahman.

Beware of bodily anger, and control thy body! Leave the sins of the body, and with thy body practise virtue!

Beware of the anger of the tongue, and control thy tongue! Leave the sins of the tongue, and practise virtue with thy tongue!

Beware of the anger of the mind, and control thy mind! Leave the sins of the mind, and practise virtue with thy mind!

The wise who control their body, who control their tongue, the wise who control their mind, are indeed well controlled.

18
Impurity

Thou art now like a sear leaf, the messengers of death, Yama, have come near to thee; thou standest at the door of thy departure, and thou hast no provision for thy journey.

Make thyself an island, work hard, be wise! When thy impurities are blown away, and thou art free from guilt, thou wilt enter into the heavenly world of the elect, Ariya.

Thy life has come to an end, thou art come near to death, Yama, there is no resting-place for thee on the road, and thou hast no provision for thy journey.

Make theyself an island, work hard, be wise! When thy impurities are blown away, and thou art free from guilt, thou wilt not enter again into birth and decay.

Let a wise man blow off the impurities of himself, as a smith blows off the impurities of silver, one by one, little by little, and from time to time.

As the impurity which springs from the iron, when it springs from it, destroys it; thus do a transgressor's own works lead him to the evil path.

The taint of prayers is, non-repetition; the taint of houses, non-repair; the taint of complexion is, sloth; the taint of a watchman, thoughtlessness.

Bad conduct is the taint of a woman, niggardliness the taint of a benefactor; tainted are all evil ways, in this world and in the next.

But there is a taint worse that all taints—ignorance is the greatest taint. O mendicants! throw off that taint, and become taintless!

Life is easy to live for a man who is without shame, a crow hero, a mischief-maker, an insulting, bold, and wretched fellow.

But life is hard to live for a modest man, who always looks for what is pure, who is disinterested, quiet, spotless, and intelligent.

He who destroys life, who speaks untruth, who in the world takes what is not given him, who goes to another man's wife;

And the man who gives himself to drinking intoxicating liquors, he, even in this world, digs up his own root.

O man, know this, that the unrestrained are in a bad state; take care that greediness

and vice do not bring thee to grief for a long time!

The world gives according to their faith or according to their pleasure: if a man frets about the food and the drink given to others, he will find no rest either by day or by night.

He in whom that feeling is destroyed, and taken out with the very root, finds rest by day and by night.

There is no fire like passion, there is no shark like hatred, there is no snare like folly, there is no torrent like greed.

The fault of others is easily perceived, but that of oneself is difficult to perceive; a man winnows his neighbour's faults like chaff, but his own fault he hides, as a cheat hides the bad die from the player.

If a man looks after the faults of others, and is always inclined to be offended, his own passions will grow, and he is far from the destruction of passion.

There is no path through the air, a man is not a Samana outwardly. The world delights in vanity, the Tathagatas are free from vanity.

There is no path through the air, a man is not a Samana outwardly. No creatures are eternal; but the Awakened, the Buddha, are never shaken.

19

The Just

A man is not just if he carries a matter by violence; no, he who distinguishes both right and wrong, who is learned and guides others, not by violence, but by the same Law, being a guardian of the Law, and intelligent, he is called just.

A man is not learned because he talks much; he who is patient, free from hatred and fear, he is called learned.

A man is not a supporter of the Law because he talks much; even if a man has learnt little, but sees the Law clearly, he is a supporter of the Law, a man who never neglects the law.

A man is not an elder because his head is grey; his age may be ripe, but he is called 'Old-in-vain.'

He in whom there is truth, virtue, piety, restraint, moderation, he who is free from impurity and is wise, he is called an elder.

An envious, stingy, dishonest man does not become respectable by means of much talking only, or by the beauty of his complexion.

He in whom all this is destroyed, and taken out with the very root, he, when freed from hatred is wise, is called respectable.

Not by tonsure does an undisciplined man who speaks falsehood become a Samana; can a man be a Samana who is still held captive by desire and greediness?

He who always quiets the evil, whether small or large, he is called a Samana, a quiet man, because he has quieted all evil.

A man is not a mendicant, Bhikshu, simply because he asks others for alms; he who adopts the whole law is a Bhikshu, not he who only begs.

He who is above good and evil, who is chaste, who with care passes through the world, he indeed is called a Bhikshu.

A man is not a Muni because he observes silence, he is foolish and ignorant; but the wise who, as with the balance, chooses the good and avoids evil, he is a Muni, and is a Muni

thereby; he who in this world weighs both sides is called a Muni.

A man is not an elect, Ariya, because he injures living creatures; because he has pity on all living creatures, therefore is a man called Ariya.

Not only by discipline and vows, not only by much learning, not by entering into a trance, not by sleeping alone, do I earn the happiness of release which no worldling can know. O Bhikshu, he who has obtained the extinction of desires, has obtained confidence.

20

The Way

The best of ways is the eightfold; the best of truths the four words; the best of virtues passionlessness; the best of men he who has eyes to see.

This is the way, there is no other that leads to the purifying of intelligence. Go on this path! This is the confusion of Mara, the tempter.

If you go on this way, you will make an end of pain! The way was preached by me, when I had understood the removal of the thorns in the flesh.

You yourself must make an effort. The Tathagatas (Buddhas) are only preachers. The thoughtful who enter the way are freed from the bondage of Mara.

'All created things perish,' he who knows and sees this becomes passive in pain; this is the way to purity.

'All created things are grief and pain,' he who knows and sees this becomes passive in pain; this is the way that leads to purity.

'All forms are unreal,' he who knows and sees this becomes passive in pain; this is the way that leads to purity.

He who does not rouse himself when it is time to rise, who, though young and strong, is full of sloth, whose will and thought are weak, that lazy and idle man never finds the way to knowledge.

Watching his speech, well restrained in mind, let a man never commit any wrong with his body! Let a man but keep these three roads of action clear, and he will achieve the way which is taught by the wise.

Through zeal knowledge is gotten, through lack of zeal knowledge is lost; let a man who knows this double path of gain and loss thus place himself that knowledge may grow.

Cut down the whole forest of desires, not a tree only! Danger comes out of the forest of desires. When you have cut down both the forest of desires and its undergrowth, then, Bhikshus, you will be rid of the forest and of desires!

So long as the desire of man towards women, even the smallest, is not destroyed, so long is his mind in bondage, as the calf that drinks milk is to its mother.

Cut out the love of self, like an autumn lotus, with thy hand! Cherish the road of peace. Nirvana has been shown by Sugata (Buddha).

'Here I shall dwell in the rain, here in winter and summer,' thus the fool meditates, and does not think of death.

Death comes and carries off that man, honoured for his children and flocks, his mind distracted, as a flood carries off a sleeping village.

Sons are no help, nor a father, nor relations; there is no help from kinsfolk for one whom death has seized.

A wise and well-behaved man who knows the meaning of this, should quickly clear the way that leads to Nirvana.

What to do?

21

The Downward Course

He who says what is not, goes to hell; he also who, having done a thing, says I have not done it. After death both are equal, they are men with evil deeds in the next world.

Many men whose shoulders are covered with the yellow gown are ill-conditioned and unrestrained; such evil-doers by their evil deeds go to hell.

Better it would be to swallow a heated iron ball, like flaring fire, than that a bad unrestrained fellow should live on the charity of the land.

Four things does a reckless man gain who covets his neighbour's wife—demerit, an uncomfortable bed, thirdly, punishment, and lastly, hell.

There is demerit, and the evil way to hell, there is the short pleasure of the frightened in the arms of the frightened, and the king imposes heavy

punishment; therefore, let no man think of his neighbour's wife.

As a grass-blade, if badly grasped, cuts the arm, badly-practised asceticism leads to hell.

An act carelessly performed, a broken vow, and hesitating obedience to Brahmachariya, all this brings no great reward.

If anything is to be done, let a man do it, let him attack it vigorously! A careless pilgrim only scatters the dust of his passions more widely.

An evil deed is better left undone, for a man repents of it afterwards; a good deed is better done, for having done it, one does not repent.

Like a well-guarded frontier fort, with defences within and without, so let a man guard himself. Not a moment should escape, for they who allow the right moment to pass, suffer pain when they are in hell.

They who are ashamed cf what they ought not to be ashamed of, and are not ashamed of what they ought to be ashamed of, such men, embracing false doctrines, enter the evil path.

They who fear when they ought not to fear, and fear not when they ought to fear, such men,

embracing false doctrines, enter the evil path.

They who see sin where there is no sin, and see no sin where there is sin, such men, embracing false doctrines, enter the evil path.

They who see sin where there is sin, and no sin where there is no sin, such men, embracing the true doctrine, enter the good path.

22

The Elephant

Silently I endured abuse as the elephant in battle endures the arrow sent from the bow: for the world is ill-natured.

They lead a tamed elephant to battle, the king mounts a tamed elephant; the tamed is the best among men, he who silently endures abuse.

Mules are good, if tamed, and noble Sindhu horses, and elephants with large tusks; but he who tames himself is better still.

For with these animals does no man reach the untrodden country, Nirvana, where a tamed man goes on a tamed animal, on his own well-tamed self.

The elephant called Dhanapalaka, his temples running with pungent sap, and who is difficult to hold, does not eat a morsel when bound; the elephant longs for the elephant grove.

If a man becomes fat and a great eater, if he is sleepy and rolls himself about, that fool, like a hog fed on grains, is born again and again.

This mind of mine went formerly wandering about as it liked, as it lusted, as it pleased; but I shall now hold it in thoroughly, as the rider who holds the hook holds in the furious elephant.

Be not thoughtless, watch your thoughts! Draw yourself out of the evil way, like an elephant sunk in mud.

If a man find a prudent companion who walks with him, is wise, and lives soberly, he may walk with him, overcoming all dangers, happy, but considerate.

If a man find no prudent companion who walks with him, is wise, and lives soberly, let him walk alone, like a king who has left his conquered country behind,—like an elephant in the forest.

It is better to live alone, there is no companionship with a fool; let a man walk alone, let him commit no sin, with few wishes, like an elephant in the forest.

If the occasion arises, friends are pleasant; enjoyment is pleasant, whatever be the cause; a

good work is pleasant in the hour of death; the giving up of all grief is pleasant.

Pleasant in the world is the state of a mother, pleasant the state of a father, pleasant the state of a Samana, pleasant the state of a Brahmin.

Pleasant is virtue lasting to old age, pleasant is a faith firmly rooted; pleasant is attainment of intelligence, pleasant is avoiding of sins.

23

Thirst

The thirst of a thoughtless man grows like a creeper; he runs from life to life, like a monkey seeking fruit in the forest.

Whomsoever this fierce poisonous thirst overcomes in this world, his sufferings increase like the abounding Birana grass.

But from him who overcomes this fierce thirst, difficult to be conquered in this world, sufferings fall off, like water-drops from a lotus leaf.

This salutary word I tell you: 'Do ye, as many as are here assembled, dig up the root of thirst, as he who wants the sweet-scented. Usira root must dig up the tough Birana grass, that Mara the tempter may not crush you again and again, as the stream crushes the reeds.'

As a tree, even though it has been cut down, is firm so long as its root is safe, and grows again,

thus, unless the feeders of thirst are destroyed, this pain of life will return again and again.

He whose thirty-six streams are strongly flowing in the channels of pleasure, the waves will carry away that misguided man, his desires which are set on passion.

The channels run everywhere, the creeper of passion stands sprouting; if you see the creeper springing up, cut its root by means of knowledge.

A creature's pleasures are extravagant and luxurious; given up to pleasure and deriving happiness, men undergo again and again birth and decay.

Beset with lust, men run about like a snared hare; held in fetters and bonds, they undergo pain for a long time, again and again.

Beset with lust, men run about like a snared hare; let therefore the mendicant drive out thirst, by striving after passionlessness for himself.

He who having got rid of the forest of lust, i.e., after having reached Nirvana gives himself over to forest-life lust, and who, when free from the forest of lust, runs to the forest to lust, look at that man! though free, he runs into bondage.

Wise people do not call that a strong fetter which is made of iron, wood, or hemp; passionately strong is the care for precious stones and rings, for sons and a wife.

That fetter wise people call strong which drags down, yields, but is difficult to undo; after having cut this at last, people leave the world, free from cares, and leaving the pleasures of love behind.

Those who are slaves to passions, run down the stream of desires, as a spider runs down the web which he has made himself; when they have cut this, at last, wise people go onwards, free from cares, leaving all pain behind.

Give up what is before, give up what is behind, give up what is between, when thou goest to the other shore of existence; if thy mind is altogether free, thou wilt not again enter into birth and decay.

If a man is tossed about by doubts, full of strong passions, and yearning only for what is delightful, his thirst will grow more and more, and he will indeed make his fetters strong.

If a man delights in quieting doubts, and, always reflecting, dwells on what is not delightful,

the impurity of the body, etc., he certainly will remove, nay, he will cut the fetter of Mara.

He who has reached the consummation, who does not tremble, who is without thirst and without sin, he has broken all the thorns of life; this will be his last body.

He who is without thirst and without affection, who understands the words and their interpretation, who knows the order of letters, those which are before and which are after, he has received his last body, he is called the great sage, the great man.

'I have conquered all, I know all, in all conditions of life I am free from taint; I have left all, and through the destruction of thirst I am free; having learnt myself, whom should I indicate as my teacher?'

The gift of the law exceeds all gifts; the sweetness of the law exceeds all sweetness; the delight in the law exceeds all delights; the extinction of thirst overcomes all pain.

Riches destroy the foolish, if they look not for the other shore; the foolish by his thirst for riches destroys himself, as if he were destroying others.

The fields are damaged by weeds, mankind is damaged by passion: therefore a gift bestowed on the passionless brings great reward.

The fields are damaged by weeds, mankind is damaged by hatred: therefore a gift bestowed on those who do not hate brings great reward.

The fields are damaged by weeds, mankind is damaged by vanity: therefore a gift bestowed on those who are free from vanity brings great reward.

The fields are damaged by weeds, mankind is damaged by lust: therefore a gift bestowed on those who are free from lust brings great reward.

A bhikshu paying homage

24
The Bhikshu

Restraint in the eye is good, good is restraint in the ear, in the nose restraint is good, good is restraint in the tongue.

In the body restraint is good, good is restraint in speech, in thought restraint is good, good is restraint in all things. A Bhikshu, restrained in all things, is freed from all pain.

He who controls his hand, he who controls his feet, he who controls his speech, he who is well controlled, he who delights inwardly, who is collected, who is solitary and content, him they call Bhikshu.

The Bhikshu who controls his mouth, who speaks wisely and calmly, who teaches the meaning and the law, his word is sweet.

He who dwells in the Law, delights in the Law, meditates on the Law, recollects the Law, that Bhikshu will never fall away from the true Law.

Let him not despise what he has received, nor ever envy others: a mendicant who envies others does not obtain peace of mind.

A Bhikshu who, though he receives little, does not despise what he has received, even the gods will praise him, if his life is pure, and if he is not slothful.

He who never identifies himself with name and form, and does not grieve over what is no more, he indeed is called a Bhikshu.

The Bhikshu who behaves with kindness, who is happy in the doctrine of Buddha, will reach the quiet place Nirvana, happiness arising from the cessation of natural inclinations.

O Bhikshu, empty this boat! if emptied, it will go quickly; having cut off passion and hatred, thou will go to Nirvana.

Cut off the five fetters, leave the five, rise above the five. A Bhikshu, who has escaped from the five fetters, he is called Oghatinna, 'saved from the flood.'

Meditate, O Bhikshu, and be not heedless! Do not direct thy thought to what gives pleasure, that thou mayest not for thy heedlessness have to

swallow the iron ball in hell, and that thou mayest not cry out when burning, 'this is pain.'

Without knowledge there is no meditation, without meditation there is no knowledge; he who has knowledge and meditation is near unto Nirvana.

A Bhikshu who has entered his empty house, and whose mind is tranquil, feels a more than human delight when he sees the law clearly.

As soon as he has considered the origin and destruction of the elements of the body, he finds happiness and joy which belong to those who know the immortal Nirvana.

And this is the beginning here for a wise Bhikshu: watchfulness over the senses, contentedness, restraint under the law; keep noble friends whose life is pure, and who are not slothful.

Let him live in charity, let him be perfect in his duties; then in the fulness of delight he will make an end of suffering.

As the Vassika plant sheds its withered flowers, men should shed passion and hatred, O Bhikshus!

The Bhikshu whose body and tongue and mind are quieted, who is collected, and has rejected the baits of the world, he is called quiet.

Rouse thyself by thyself, examine thyself by thyself, thus self-protected and attentive wilt thou live happily, O Bhikshu!

For self is the lord of self, self is the refuge of self; therefore curb thyself as the merchant curbs a noble horse.

The Bhikshu, full of delight, who is happy in the doctrine of Buddha, will reach the quiet place, Nirvana, happiness consisting in the cessation of natural inclinations.

He who, even as a young Bhikshu, applies himself to the doctrine of Buddha, brightens up this world, like the moon when free from clouds.

25
The Brahmin

Stop the stream valiantly, drive away the desires, O Brahmin! When you have understood the destruction of all that was made, you will understand that which was not made.

If the Brahmin has reached the other shore in both Laws, in restraint and contemplation, all bonds vanish from him who has obtained knowledge.

He for whom there is neither the hither nor the further shore, nor both, him, the fearless and unshackled, I call indeed a Brahmin.

He who is thoughtful, blameless, settled, dutiful, without passions, and who has attained the highest end, him I call indeed a Brahmin.

The sun is bright by day, the moon shines by night, the warrior is bright in his armour, the Brahmin is bright in his meditation; but Buddha, the Awakened, is bright with splendour day and night.

Because a man is rid of evil, therefore he is called Brahmin; because he walks quietly, therefore he is called Samana; because he has sent away his own impurities, therefore he is called Pravrajita, a pilgrim.

No one should attack a Brahmin, but no Brahmin if attacked should let himself fly at his aggressor! Woe to him who strikes a Brahmin, more woe to him who flies at his aggressor!

It advantages a Brahmin not a little if he holds his mind back from the pleasures of life; the more all wish to injure has vanished, the more all pain will cease.

Him I call indeed a Brahmin who does not offend by body, word, or thought, and is controlled on these three points.

He from whom he may learn the law, as taught by the Well-awakened, the Buddha, him, let him worship assiduously, as the Brahmin worships the sacrificial fire.

A man does not become a Brahmin by his plaited hair, by his family, or by birth; in whom there is truth and righteousness, he is blessed, he is a Brahmin.

What is the use of platted hair, O fool!

what of the raiment of goat-skins? Within thee there is ravening, but the outside thou makest clean.

The man who wears dirty raiments, who is emaciated and covered with veins, who meditates alone in the forest, him I call indeed a Brahmin.

I do not call a man a Brahmin because of his origin or of his mother. He is indeed arrogant, and he is wealthy: but the poor, who is free from all attachments, him I call indeed a Brahmin.

Him I call indeed a Brahmin who after cutting all fetters never trembles, is free from bonds and unshackled.

Him I call indeed a Brahmin who after cutting the strap and the thong, the rope with all that pertains to it, has destroyed all obstacles, and is awakened.

Him I call indeed a Brahmin who, though he has committed no offence, endures reproach, stripes, and bonds, who has endurance for his force, and strength for his army.

Him I call indeed a Brahmin who is free from anger, dutiful, virtuous, without appetites, who is subdued, and has received his last body.

Him I call indeed a Brahmin who does not cling to sensual pleasures, like water on a lotus leaf, like a mustard seed on the point of a needle.

Him I call indeed a Brahmin who, even here, knows the end of his own suffering, has put down his burden, and is unshackled.

Him I call indeed a Brahmin whose knowledge is deep, who possesses wisdom, who knows the right way and the wrong, and has attained the highest end.

Him I call indeed a Brahmin who keeps aloof both from laymen and from mendicants, who frequents no houses, and has but few desires.

Him I call indeed a Brahmin who without hurting any creatures, whether feeble or strong, does not kill nor cause slaughter.

Him I call indeed a Brahmin who is tolerant with the intolerant, mild with the violent, and free from greed among the greedy.

Him I call indeed a Brahmin from whom anger and hatred, pride and hypocrisy have dropt like a mustard seed from the point of a needle.

Him I call indeed a Brahmin who utters true

speech, instructive and free from harshness, so that he offend no one.

Him I call indeed a Brahmin who takes nothing in the world that is not given him, be it long or short, small or large, good or bad.

Him I call indeed a Brahmin who fosters no desires for this world or for the next, has no inclinations, and is unshackled.

Him I call indeed a Brahmin who has no interests, and when he has understood the truth, does not say How, how? and who has reached the depth of the Immortal.

Him I call indeed a Brahmin who in this world has risen above both ties, good and evil, who is free from grief, from sin, and from impurity.

Him I call indeed a Brahmin who is high like the moon, pure, serene, undisturbed, and in whom all gaiety is extinct.

Him I call indeed a Brahmin who has traversed this miry road, the impassable world, difficult to pass, and its vanity, who has gone through, and reached the other shore, is thoughtful, steadfast, free from doubts, free from attachment, and content.

Him I call indeed a Brahmin who in this world having abandoned all desires, travels about

without a home, and in whom all concupiscence is extinct.

Him I call indeed a Brahmin who, having abandoned all longings, travels about without a home, and in whom all covetousness is extinct.

Him I call indeed a Brahmin who, after leaving all bondage to men, has risen above all bondage to the gods, and is free from all and every bondage.

Him I call indeed a Brahmin who has left what gives pleasure and what gives pain, who is cold, and free from all germs of renewed life the hero who has conquered all the worlds.

Him I call indeed a Brahmin who knows the destruction and the return of beings everywhere, who is free from bondage, welfaring (Sugata) and awakened (Buddha).

Him I call indeed a Brahmin whose path gods do not know, nor Gandharvas, nor men, whose passions are extinct, and who is an Arhat.

Him I call indeed a Brahmin who calls nothing his own, whether it be before, behind, or between, who is poor, and free from the love of the world.

Him I call indeed a Brahmin, the manly, the noble, the hero, the great sage, the conqueror, the indifferent, the accomplished, the awakened.

Him I call indeed a Brahmin who knows his former abodes, who sees heaven and hell, has reached the end of births, is perfect in knowledge, a sage, and whose perfections are all perfect.

26

Miscellaneous

If by leaving a small pleasure one sees a great pleasure, let a wise man leave the small pleasure, and look to the great.

He who, by causing pain to others, wishes to obtain pleasure for himself, he, entangled in the bonds of hatred, will never be free from hatred.

What ought to be done is neglected, what ought not to be done is done; the desires of unruly, thoughtless people are always increasing.

But they whose whole watchfulness is always directed to their body, who do not follow what ought not to be done, and who steadfastly do what ought to be done, the desires of such watchful and wise people will come to an end.

A true Brahmin goes scathless, though he has killed father and mother, and two valiant kings, though he has destroyed a kingdom with all its subjects.

A true Brahmin goes scatheless, though he has killed father and mother, and two holy kings, and an eminent man besides.

The disciples of Gotama Buddha are always well awake, and their thoughts day and night are always set on Buddha.

The disciples of Gotama are always well awake, and their thoughts day and night are always set on the Law.

The disciples of Gotama are always well awake, and their thoughts day and night are always set on the Sangh.

The disciples of Gotama are always well awake, and their thoughts day and night are always set on their body.

The disciples of Gotama are always well awake, and their mind day and night always delights in compassion.

The disciples of Gotama are always well awake, and their mind day and night always delights in meditation.

It is hard to leave the world to become a friar, it is hard to enjoy the world; hard is the monastery, painful are the houses; painful it is to dwell with

equals to share everything in common, and the itinerant mendicant is beset with pain. Therefore let no man be an itinerant mendicant, and he will not be beset with pain.

A man full of faith, if endowed with virtue and glory, is respected, whatever place he may choose.

Good people shine from afar, like the snowy mountains; bad people are not seen, like arrows shot by night.

Sitting alone, lying down alone, walking alone without ceasing, and alone subduing himself, let a man be happy near the edge of a forest.

Peace be!

BUDDHA MEDITATIONS

AMITAYUR-DHYANA SUTRA

Translated by
F. Max Muller

The Sutra

According to the Buddhists of Japan, Buddha preached the Amitayur-dhyana Sutra to queen Vaidehi in the city of Rajagriha. This was during the fifth period of his life, when he was seventy nine.

Vaidehi, consort of king Bimbisara of Magadha, seeing the wicked actions of his son, Ajatasatru, began to feel weary of this world; Sakyamuni then taught her how to be born in the pure land Sukhavati, instructing her in the method of being born in that world, enumerating three kinds of good actions. The first is worldly goodness, which includes good actions in general, such as filial piety, respect for elders, loyalty, faithfulness, etc. The second is the goodness of Sila or morality, in which there are differences between the priesthood and the laity. In short, however, all who do not oppose the general rule

of reproving wickedness and exhorting to the practice of virtue are included in this goodness.

The third is the goodness of practice, which includes that of the four satyas or truths, and the six paramitas or perfections. Besides these, all other pure and good actions, such as the reading and recital of the Mahayana Sutras, persuading others to hear the Law, and thirteen kinds of goodness to be practised by fixed thought, are comprised in this.

Towards the end of the Sutra, Buddha says: 'Let not one's voice cease, but ten times complete the thought, and reapeat and words 'Namo Mitabhaya Buddhaya', or Adoration to Amitabha Buddha. This practice is most excellent of all.

Oxford –F. Max Muller
Jan 26, 1894

The Buddha of Light, at Nara, Japan.
53½ feet in height.

Buddha Meditations

1

Thus it was heard by me:

At one time—the Buddha dwelt in Rajagriha, on the mountain Gridhrakuta, with a large assembly of Bhikshus and with thirty-two thousands of Bodhisattvas; with Manjusri, Prince of the Law, at the head of the assembly.

At that time, in the great city of Rajagriha there was a prince, the heir-apparent, named Ajatasatru. He listened to the wicked counsel of Devadatta and other friends and forcibly arrested Bimbisara his father, the king, and shut him up by himself in a room with seven walls, proclaiming to all the courtiers that no one should approach the king.

The chief consort of the king, Vaidehi by name, was true and faithful to her lord, the king. She supported him in this wise: having purified

herself by bathing and washing, she anointed her body with honey and ghee mixed with corn-flour, and she concealed the juice of grapes in the various garlands she wore in order to give him food without being noticed by the warder. As she stole in and made an offering to him, he was able to eat the flour and to drink the juice of grapes. Then he called for water and rinsed his mouth.

That done, the king stretched forth his folded hands towards the Mount Gridhrakuta and worshipped duly and respectfully the World-Honoured One, who at that time abode there. And he uttered the following prayer: 'Mahamaudgalyayana is my friend and relative; let him, I pray, feel compassion towards me, and come and communicate to me the eight prohibitive precepts of Buddha.' On this, Mahamaudgalyayana at once appeared before the king, coming with a speed equal to the flight of a falcon or an eagle, and communicated to him the eight precepts.

Day after day did he come. The World-Honoured One sent also his worthy disciple Purna to preach the Law to the king. Thus a period of three weeks passed by. The king showed by his

countenance that he was happy and contented when he had an opportunity of hearing the Law as well as of enjoying the honey and flour.

At that time, Ajatasatru asked the warder of the gate whether his father was yet alive. On this, the warder answered him: 'O Exalted King, the chief consort of thy father brought food and presented it to him by anointing her body with honey and flour and filling her garlands with the juice of grapes, and the Sramanas, Mahamaudgalyayana and Purna, approached the king through the sky in order to preach the Law to him. It is O king, impossible to prevent them coming.'

When the prince heard this answer his indignation arose against his mother: 'My mother,' he cried, 'is, indeed, a rebel, for she was found in company with that rebel. Wicked people are those Sramanas, and it is their art of spells causing illusion and delusion that delayed the death of that wicked king for so many days.' Instantly he brandished his sharp sword, intending to slay his mother.

At that moment, there intervened a minister named Chandraprabha, who was possessed of

great wisdom and intelligence, and Jiva, the famous physician. They saluted the prince and remonstrated with him, saying: 'We, ministers, O Great King, heard that since the beginning of the kalpas there had been several wicked kings, even to the number of eighteen thousand, who killed their own fathers, coveting the throne of their respective kingdoms, as mentioned in the Sutra of the discourse of the Veda. Yet never have we heard of a man killing his mother, though he be void of virtue. Now, if thou, O King, shouldst dare to commit such a deadly sin, thou wouldst bring a stain upon the blood of the Kshatriyas. We cannot even bear to hear of it. Thou art indeed a Chandala, the lowest race; we shall not stay here with thee.'

After this speech, the two great ministers retired stepping backward, each with his hand placed on his sword.

Ajatasatru was then frightened, and greatly afraid of them, and asked Jiva, saying: 'Wilt thou not be friendly to me?' In reply Jiva said to him: 'Do not then, O Great King, by any means think of injuring thy mother.' On hearing this, the prince repented and sought for mercy, and at once

laid down his sword and did his mother no hurt. He finally ordered the officers of the inner chambers to put the queen in a hidden palace and not to allow her to come out again.

When Vaidehi was thus shut up in retirement, she became afflicted by sorrow and distress. She began to do homage to Buddha from afar, looking towards the Mount Gridhrakuta. She uttered the following words: 'O Tathagata! World-Honoured One! In former times thou hast constantly sent Ananda to me for enquiry and consolation. I am now in sorrow and grief. Thou, O World-Honoured One, art majestic and exalted; in no way shall I be able to see thee. Wilt thou, I pray thee, command Mahamaudgalyayana and thy honoured disciple Ananda, to come and have an interview with me?' After this speech, she grieved and wept, shedding tears like a shower of rain.

Before she raised her head from doing homage to the distant Buddha, the World-Honoured One knew what Vaidehi was wishing in her mind, though he was on the Mount Gridhrakuta. Therefore, he instantly ordered Mahamaudgalyayana and Ananda to go to her

through the sky. Buddha himself disappeared from that mountain and appeared in the royal palace.

When the queen raised her head as she finished homage to Buddha, she saw before her the W orld-Honoured Buddha Sakyamuni, whose body was purple gold in colour, sitting on a lotus flower which consists of a hundred jewels, with Mahamaudgalyayana attending on his left, and with Ananda on his right. Sakra (Indra), Brahma, and other gods that protect the world, were seen in the midst of the sky, everywhere showering heavenly flowers with which they made offerings to Buddha in their worship. Vaidehi, at the sight of Buddha, the World-Honoured One, took off her garlands and prostrated herself on the ground, crying, sobbing, and speaking to Buddha: 'O World-Honoured One! What former sin of mine has produced such a wicked son? And again, O Exalted One, from what cause and circumstances hast thou such an affinity by blood and religion with Devadatta (Buddha's wicked cousin and once his disciple)?'

'My only prayer,' she continued, 'is this: O World-Honoured One, mayst thou preach to me in detail of all the places where there is no sorrow

or trouble, and where I ought to go to be born anew. I am not satisfied with this world of depravities, with Jambudvipa (India), which is full of hells, full of hungry spirits, pretas', and of the brute creation. In this world of depravities, there is many an assemblage of the wicked. May I not hear, I pray, the voice of the wicked in the future; and may I not see any wicked person.

'Now I throw my five limbs down to the ground before thee, and seek for thy mercy by confessing my sins. I pray for this only that the sunlike Buddha may instruct me how to meditate on a world wherein all actions are pure.'

At that moment, the World-Honoured One flashed forth a golden ray from between his eyebrows. It extended to all the innumerable worlds of the ten quarters. On its return the ray rested on the top of Buddha's head and transformed itself into a golden pillar just like the Mount Sumeru, wherein the pure and admirable countries of the Buddhas in the ten quarters appeared all at once illuminated.

One was a country consisting of seven jewels, another was a country all full of lotus flowers; one was like the palace of Mahesvara Deva,

another was like a mirror of crystal, with the countries in the ten quarters reflected therein. There were innumerable countries like these, resplendent, gorgeous, and delightful to look upon. All were meant for Vaidehi to see and choose from.

Thereupon Vaidehi again spoke to Buddha: 'O World-Honoured One, although all other Buddha countries are pure and radiant with light, I should, nevertheless, wish myself to be born in the realm of Buddha Amitayus (Amitabha), in the world of Highest Happiness, Sukhavati. Now I simply pray thee, O World-Honoured One, to teach me how to concentrate my thought so as to obtain a right vision of that country.'

Thereupon the World-Honoured One gently smiled upon her, and rays of five colours issued forth out of his mouth, each ray shining as far as the head of king Bimbisara.

At that moment, the mental vision of that exalted king was perfectly clear though he was shut up in lonely retirement, and he could see the World-Honoured One from afar. As he paid homage with his head and face, he naturally increased and advanced in wisdom, whereby he

attained to the fruition of an Anagamin, the third of the four grades to Nirvana.

Then the World-Honoured One said: 'Now dost thou not know, O Vaidehi, that Buddha Amitayus is not very far from here? Thou shouldst apply thy mind entirely to close meditation upon those who have already perfected the pure actions necessary for that Buddha country.

'I now proceed to fully expound them for thee in many parables, and thereby afford all ordinary persons of the future who wish to cultivate these pure actions an opportunity of being born in the Land of Highest Happiness, Sukhavati in the western quarter. Those who wish to be born in that country of Buddha have to cultivate a threefold goodness. Firstly, they should act filially towards their parents and support them; serve and respect their teachers and elders; be of compassionate mind, abstain from doing any injury, and cultivate the ten virtuous actions. Secondly, they should take and observe the vow of seeking refuge with the Three Jewels, fulfil all moral precepts, and not lower their dignity or neglect any ceremonial observance. Thirdly, they should give their whole mind to the attainment

of the Bodhi, perfect wisdom, deeply believe in the principle of cause and effect, study and recite the Sutras of the Mahayana doctrine, and persuade and encourage others who pursue the same course as themselves.

'These three groups as enumerated are called the pure actions leading to the Buddha country: O Vaidehi!' Buddha continued, 'dost thou not understand now? These three classes of actions are the efficient cause of the pure actions taught by all the Buddhas of the past, present, and future.'

Buddha then addressed Ananda as well as Vaidehi: 'Listen carefully, listen carefully! Ponder carefully on what you hear! I, Tathagata, now declare the pure actions needful for that Buddha country for the sake of all beings hereafter, that are subject to the misery inflicted by the enemy, i.e., passion. Well done, O Vaidehi! Appropriate questions are those which thou hast asked! O Ananda, do thou remember these words of me, of Buddha, and repeat them openly to many assemblies. I, Tathagata, now teach Vaidehi and also all beings hereafter in order that they may meditate on the World of Highest Happiness Sukhavati in the western quarter.

'It is by the power of Buddha only that one can see that pure land of Buddha as clear as one sees the image of one's face reflected in the transparent mirror held up before one.

'When one sees the state of happiness of that country in its highest excellence, one greatly rejoices in one's heart and immediately attains a spirit of resignation prepared to endure whatever consequences may yet arise.'

Buddha, turning again to Vaidehi, said: 'Thou art but an ordinary person; the quality of thy mind is feeble and inferior. Thou hast not as yet obtained the divine eye and canst yet perceive what is at a distance. All the Buddhas, Tathagatas, have various means at their disposal and can therefore afford thee an opportunity of seeing that Buddha country.'

Then Vaidehi rejoined: 'O World-Honoured One, people such as I, can now see that land by the power of Buddha, but how shall all those beings who are to come after Buddha's nirvana, and who, as being depraved and devoid of good qualities, will be harassed by the five worldly sufferings—how shall they see the World of Highest Happiness of the Buddha Amitayus?'

2

Buddha then replied: 'Thou and all other beings besides ought to make it their only aim, with concentrated thought, to get a perception of the western quarter. You will ask how that perception is to be formed. I will explain it now. All beings, if not blind from birth, are uniformly possessed of sight, and they all see the setting sun. Thou shouldst sit down properly, looking in the western direction, and prepare thy thought for a close meditation on the sun; cause thy mind to be firmly fixed on it so as to have an unwavering perception by the exclusive application of thy thought, and gaze upon it more particularly when it is about to set and looks like a suspended drum.

'After thou hast thus seen the sun, let that image remain clear and fixed, whether thine eyes be shut or open;—such is perception of the sun, which is the **First Meditation**.

Next thou shouldst form the perception of water; gaze on the water clear and pure, and let this image also remain clear and fixed afterward; never allow thy thought to be scattered and lost.

'When thou hast thus seen the water thou shouldst form the perception of ice. As thou seest the ice shining and transparent, thou shouldst imagine the appearance of lapis lazuli.

'After that has been done, thou wilt see the ground consisting of lapis lazuli, transparent and shining both within and without. Beneath this ground of lapis lazuli there will be seen a golden banner with the seven jewels, diamonds and the rest, supporting the ground. It extends to the eight points of the compass, and thus the eight corners of the ground are perfectly filled up. Every side of the eight quarters consists of a hundred jewels, every jewel has a thousand rays, and every ray has eighty-four thousand colours which, when reflected in the ground of lapis lazuli, look like a thousand millions of suns, and it is difficult to see them all one by one. Over the surface of that ground of lapis lazuli there are stretched golden ropes intertwined crosswise; divisions are made by means of strings of seven jewels with every part clear and distinct.

'Each jewel has rays of five hundred colours which look like flowers or like the moon and stars. Lodged high up in the open sky these rays form a

Look inside!

tower of rays, whose storeys and galleries are ten millions in number and built of a hundred jewels. Both sides of the tower have each a hundred millions of flowery banners furnished and decked with numberless musical instruments. Eight kinds of cool breezes proceed from the brilliant rays. When those musical instruments are played, they emit the sounds "suffering," "non-existence," "impermanence:" and "non-self;"—such is the perception of the water, which is the **Second Meditation**.

'When this perception has been formed, thou shouldst meditate on its constituents one by one and make the images as clear as possible, so that they may never be scattered and lost, whether thine eyes be shut or open. Except only during the time of thy sleep, thou shouldst always keep this in thy mind. One who has reached this stage of perception is said to have dimly seen the Land of Highest Happiness, Sukhavati.

'One who has obtained the Samadhi is able to see the land; of that Buddha country clearly and distinctly: this state is too much to be explained fully;—such is the perception of the land, and it is the **Third Meditation**.

'Thou shouldst remember, O Ananda, the Buddha words of mine, and repeat this law for attaining to the perception of the land of the Buddha country for the sake of the great mass of the people hereafter who may wish to be delivered from their sufferings. If anyone meditates on the land of that Buddha country, his sins which bind him to births and deaths during eighty millions of kalpas shall be expiated; after the abandonment of his present body, he will assuredly be born in the pure land in the following life. The practice of this kind of meditation is called the "right meditation." If it be of another kind it is called "heretical meditation."'

Buddha then spoke to Ananda and Vaidehi: 'When the perception of the land of that Buddha country has been gained, you should next meditate on the jewel-trees of that country. In meditating on the jewel-trees, you should take each by itself and form a perception of the seven rows of trees; every tree is eight hundred yojanas high, and all the jewel-trees have flowers and leaves consisting of seven jewels all perfect. All flowers and leaves have colours like the colours of various jewels:—from the colour of lapis lazuli there issues

a golden ray; from the colour of crystal, a saffron ray; from the colour of agate, a diamond ray; from the colour of diamond, a ray of blue pearls. Corals, amber, and all other gems are used as ornaments for illumination; nets of excellent pearls are spread over the trees, each tree is covered by seven sets of nets, and between one set and another there are five hundred millions of palaces built of excellent flowers, resembling the palace of the Lord Brahma; all heavenly children live there quite naturally; every child has a garland consisting of five hundred millions of precious gems like those that are fastened on Sakra's head, the rays of which shine over a hundred yojanas, just as if a hundred millions of suns and moons were united together; it is difficult to explain them in detail. That garland is the most excellent among all, as it is the commixture of all sorts of jewels. Rows of these jewel-trees touch one another; the leaves of the trees also join one another.

'Among the dense foliage there blossom various beautiful flowers, upon which are miraculously found fruits of seven jewels. The leaves of the trees are all exactly equal in length and in breadth, measuring twenty-five Yojanas each way; every leaf has a thousand colours and a

hundred different pictures on it, just like a heavenly garland. There are many excellent flowers which have the colour of Jambunada gold and an appearance of fire-wheels in motion, turning between the leaves in a graceful fashion. All the fruits are produced just as easily as if they flowed out from the pitcher of the god Sakra. There is a magnificent ray which transforms itself into numberless jewelled canopies with banners and flags. Within these jewelled canopies the works of all the Buddhas of the Great Chiliocosm appear illuminated; the Buddha countries of the ten quarters also are manifested therein. When you have seen these trees you should also meditate on them one by one in order. In meditating on the trees, trunks, branches, leaves, flowers, and fruits, let them all be distinct and clear;—such is the perception of the trees of that Buddha country, and it is the **Fourth Meditation.**

'Next, you should percieive the water of that country. The perception of the water is as follows:

'In the Land of Highest Happiness there are waters in eight lakes; the water in every lake

consists of seven jewels which are soft and yielding. Deriving its source from the king of jewels that fulfils every wish, the water is divided into fourteen streams; every stream has the colour of seven jewels; its channel is built of gold, the bed of which consists of the sand of variegated diamonds.

'In the midst of each lake there are sixty millions of lotus flowers, made of seven jewels; all the flowers are perfectly round and exactly equal in circumference, being twelve yojanas. The water of jewels flows amidst the flowers and rises and falls by the stalks of the lotus; the sound of the streaming water is melodious and pleasing, and propounds all the perfect virtues, Paramitas, "suffering," "non-existence," "impermanence," and "non-self;" it proclaims also the praise of the signs of perfection, and minor marks of excellence of all Buddhas. From the king of jewels that fulfils every wish, stream forth the golden-coloured rays excessively beautiful, the radiance of which transforms itself into birds possessing the colours of a hundred jewels, which sing out harmonious notes, sweet and delicious, ever praising the remembrance of Buddha, the remembrance of the

Law, and the remembrance of the Church;—such is the perception of the water of eight good qualities, and it is the **Fifth Meditation.**

'Each division of that Buddha country, which consists of several jewels, has also jewelled storeys and galleries to the number of five hundred millions; within each storey and gallery there are innumerable Devas engaged in playing heavenly music. There are some musical instruments that are hung up in the open sky, like the jewelled banners of heaven; they emit musical sounds without being struck, which, while resounding variously, all propound the remembrance of Buddha, of the Law and of the Church, Bhikshus, etc. When this perception is duly accomplished, one is said to have dimly seen the jewel-trees, jewel-ground, and jewel-lakes of that World of Highest Happiness, Sukhavati;—such is the perception formed by meditating on the general features of that Land, and it is the **Sixth Meditation.**

If one has experienced this, one has expiated the greatest sinful deeds which would otherwise lead one to transmigration for numberless millions

of kalpas; after his death he will assuredly be born in that land.

'Listen carefully! listen carefully! Think over what you have heard! I, Buddha, am about to explain in detail the law of delivering one's self from trouble and torment. Commit this to your memory in order to explain it in detail before a great assembly.'

While Buddha was uttering these words, Buddha Amitayus stood in the midst of the sky with Bodhisattvas Mahasthama and Avalokitesvara, attending on his right and left respectively. There was such a bright and dazzling radiance that no one could see clearly; the brilliance was a thousand times greater than that of gold Jambunada. Thereupon Vaidehi saw Buddha Amitayus and approached the World-Honoured One, and worshipped him, touching his feet; and spoke to him as follows: 'O Exalted One! I am now able, by the power of Buddha, to see Buddha Amitayus together with the two Bodhisattvas. But how shall all the beings of the future meditate on Buddha Amitayus and the two Bodhisattvas?'

Buddha answered: 'Those who wish to meditate on that Buddha ought first to direct their

thought as follows: form the perception of a lotus flower on a ground of seven jewels, each leaf of that lotus exhibits the colours of a hundred jewels, and has eighty-four thousand veins, just like heavenly pictures; each vein possesses eighty-four thousand rays, of which each can be clearly seen. Every small leaf and flower is two hundred and fifty yojanas in length and the same measure-ment in breadth. Each lotus flower possesses eighty-four thousand leaves, each leaf has the kingly pearls to the number of a hundred millions, as ornaments for illumination; each pearl shoots out a thousand rays like bright canopies. The surface of the ground is entirely covered by a mixture of seven jewels. There is a tower built of the gems which are like those that are fastened on Sakra's head. It is inlaid and decked with eighty thousand diamonds, Kimsuka jewels, Brahma-mani and excellent pearl nets.

'On that tower there are miraculously found four posts with jewelled banners; each banner looks like a hundred thousand millions of Sumeru mountains.

'The jewelled veil over these banners is like that of the celestial palace of Yama, illuminated

with five hundred millions of excellent jewels, each jewel has eighty-four thousand rays, each ray has various golden colours to the number of eighty-four thousand, each golden colour covers the whole jewelled soil, it changes and is transformed at various places, every now and then exhibiting various appearances; now it becomes a diamond tower, now a pearl net, again clouds of mixed flowers, freely changing its manifestation in the ten directions it exhibits the state of Buddha;—such is the perception of the flowery throne, and it is the **Seventh Meditation.**'

Buddha, turning to Ananda, said: 'These excellent flowers were created originally by the power of the prayer of Bhikshu Dharmakara. All who wish to exercise the remembrance of that Buddha ought first to form the perception of that flowery throne. When engaged in it one ought not to perceive vaguely, but fix the mind upon each detail separately. Leaf, jewel, ray, tower, and banner should be clear and distinct, just as one sees the image of one's own face in a mirror. When one has achieved this perception, the sins which would produce births and deaths during fifty thousand kalpas are expiated, and he is one who

will most assuredly be born in the World of Highest Happiness.

'When you have perceived this, you should next perceive Buddha himself. Do you ask how? Every Buddha Tathagata is one whose spiritual body is the principle of nature Darmadhatukaya, so that he may enter into the mind of any being. Consequently, when you have perceived Buddha, it is indeed that mind of yours that possesses those thirty-two signs of perfection and eighty minor marks of excellence; which you see in Buddha. In fine, it is your mind that becomes Buddha, nay, it is your mind that is indeed Buddha. The ocean of true and universal knowledge of all the Buddhas derives its source from one's own mind and thought. Therefore, you should apply your thought with an undivided attention to a careful meditation on that Buddha Tathagata, Arhat, the Holy and Fully Enlightened One. In forming the perception of that Buddha, you should first perceive the image of that Buddha; whether your eyes be open or shut, look at an image like Jambunada gold in colour, sitting on that flower throne.

'When you have seen the seated figure your mental vision will become clear, and you will be able to see clearly and distinctly the adornment of that Buddha country, the jewelled ground, etc. In seeing these things, let them be clear and fixed just as you see the palms of your hands. When you have passed through this experience, you should further form a perception of another great lotus flower which is on the left side of Buddha, and is exactly equal in every way to the above-mentioned lotus flower of Buddha. Still further, you should form a perception of another lotus flower which is on the right side of Buddha. Perceive that an image of Bodhisattva Avalokitesvara is sitting on the left-hand flowery throne, shooting forth golden rays exactly like those of Buddha. Perceive then that an image of Bodhisattva Mahasthama is sitting on the right-hand flowery throne.

When these perceptions are gained the images of Buddha and the Bodhisattvas will all send forth brilliant rays, clearly lighting up all the jewel-trees with golden colour. Under every tree there are also three lotus flowers. On every lotus flower there is an image, either of Buddha or of a

Yes, I can see!

Bodhisattva; thus the images of the Bodhisattvas and of Buddha are found everywhere in that country.

'When this perception has been gained, the devotee should hear the excellent Law preached by means of a stream of water, a brilliant ray of light, several jewel-trees, ducks, geese, and swans. Whether he be wrapped in meditation or whether he has ceased from it, he should ever hear the excellent Law. What the devotee hears must be kept in memory and not be lost, when he ceases from that meditation; and it should agree with the Sutras, for if it does not agree with the Sutras, it is called an illusory perception, whereas if it does agree, it is called the rough perception of the World of Highest Happiness;—such is the perception of the images, and it is the **Eighth Meditation**.

'He who has practised this meditation is freed from the sins which otherwise involve him in births and deaths for innumerable millions of kalpas, and during this present life he obtains the Samadhi due to the remembrance of Buddha.

'Further, when this perception is gained, you should next proceed to meditate on the bodily marks and the light of Buddha Amitayus.

'Thou shouldst know, O Ananda, that the body of Buddha Amitayus is hundred thousand million times as bright as the colour of the Jambunada gold of the heavenly abode of Yama; the height of that Buddha is six hundred thousand niyutas of kotis of yojanas innumerable as are the sands of the river Ganga.

'The white twist of hair between the eyebrows all turning to the right, is just like the five Sumeru mountains.

'The eyes of Buddha are like the water of the four great oceans; the blue and the white are quite distinct.

'All the roots of hair of his body issue forth brilliant rays which are also like the Sumeru mountains.

'The halo of that Buddha is like a hundred millions of the Great Chiliocosms; in that halo there are Buddhas miraculously created, to the number of a million of niyutas of kotis innumerable as the sands of the Ganga; each of

these Buddhas has for attendants a great assembly of numberless Bodhisattvas who are also miraculously created.

'Buddha Amitayus has eighty-four thousand signs of perfection, each sign is possessed of eighty-four minor marks of excellence, each mark has eighty-four thousand rays, each ray extends so far as to shine over the worlds of the ten quarters, whereby Buddha embraces and protects all the beings who think upon him and does not exclude anyone of them. His rays, signs, etc., are difficult to be explained in detail. But in simple meditation let the mind's eye dwell upon them.

'If you pass through this experience, you will at the same time see all the Buddhas of the ten quarters. Since you see all the Buddhas it is called the Samadhi of the remembrance of the Buddhas.

'Those who have practised this meditation are said to have contemplated the bodies of all the Buddhas. Since they have meditated on Buddha's body, they will also see Buddha's mind. It is great compassion that is called Buddha's mind. It is by his absolute compassion that he receives all beings.

'Those who have practised this meditation will, when they die, be born in the presence of the Buddhas in another life, and obtain a spirit of resignation wherewith to face all the consequences which shall hereafter arise.

'Therefore, those who have wisdom should direct their thought to the careful meditation upon that Buddha Amitayus. Let those who meditate on Buddha Amitayus begin with one single sign or mark—let them first meditate on the white twist of hair between the eyebrows as clearly as possible; when they have done this, the eighty-four thousand signs and marks will naturally appear before their eyes. Those who see Amitayus will also see all the innumerable Buddhas of the ten quarters. Since they have seen all the innumerable Buddhas, they will receive the prophecy of their future destiny to become Buddha, in the presence of all the Buddhas;—such is the perception gained by a complete meditation on all forms and bodies of Buddha, and it is the **Ninth Meditation.**

'When you have seen Buddha Amitayus distinctly, you should then further meditate upon Bodhisattva Avalokitesvara, whose height is eight

hundred thousands of niyutas of yojanas; the colour of his body is purple gold, his head has a turban, at the back of which there is a halo; the circumference of his face is a hundred thousand yojanas. In that halo, there are five hundred Buddhas miraculously transformed just like those of Sakyamuni Buddha, each transformed Buddha is attended by five hundred transformed Bodhisattvas who are also attended by numberless gods.

'Within the circle of light emanating from his whole body, appear illuminated the various forms and marks of all beings that live in the five paths of existence.

'On the top of his head is a heavenly crown of gems like those that are fastened on Indra's head, in which crown there is a transformed Buddha standing, twenty-five yojanas high.

'The face of Bodhisattva Avalokitesvara is like Jambutnada gold in colour.

'The soft hair between the eyebrows has all the colours of the seven jewels, from which eighty-four kinds of rays flow out, each ray has innumerable transformed Buddhas, each of whom is attended by numberless transformed Bodhis-

attvas; freely changing their manifestations they fill up the worlds of the ten quarters; the appearance can be compared with the colour of the red lotus flower.

'He wears a garland consisting of eight thousand rays, in which is seen fully reflected a state of perfect beauty. The palm of his hand has a mixed colour of five hundred lotus flowers. His hands have ten tips of fingers, each tip has eighty-four thousand pictures, which are like signet-marks, each picture has eighty-four thousand colours, each colour has eighty-four thousand rays which are soft and mild and shine over all things that exist. With these jewel hands he draws and embraces all beings. When he lifts up his feet, the soles of his feet are seen to be marked with a wheel of a thousand spokes one of the thirty-two signs which miraculously transform themselves into five hundred million pillars of rays. When he puts his feet down to the ground, the flowers of diamonds and jewels are scattered about, and all things are simply covered by them. All the other signs of his body and the minor marks of excellence are perfect, and not at all different from those of

Buddha, except the signs of having the turban on his head and the top of his head invisible, which two signs of him are inferior to those of the World-Honoured One;—such is the perception of the real form and body of Bodhisattva Avalokitesvara, and it is the **Tenth Meditation**.'

Buddha, especially addressing Ananda, said: 'Whosoever wishes to meditate on Bodhisattva Avalokitesvara must do so in the way I have explained. Those who practise this meditation will not suffer any calamity; they will utterly remove the obstacle that is raised by Karma, and will expiate the sins which would involve them in births and deaths for numberless kalpas. Even the hearing of the name of this Bodhisattva will enable one to obtain immeasurable happiness. How much more, then, will the diligent contemplation of him!

'Whosoever will meditate on Bodhisattva Avalokitesvara should first meditate on the turban of his head, and then on his heavenly crown.

'All the other signs should also be meditated on according to their order, and they should be

dear and distinct just as one sees the palms of one's hands.

'Next you should meditate on Bodhisattva Mahasthama, whose body signs, height, and size are equal to those of Avalokitesvara; the circumference of his halo is one hundred and twenty-five yojanas, and it shines as far as two hundred and fifty yojanas. The rays of his whole body shine over the countries of the ten quarters, they are purple gold in colour, and can be seen by all beings that are in favourable circumstances.

'If one but sees the ray that issues from a single root of the hair of this Bodhisattva, he will at the same time see the pure and excellent rays of all the innumerable Buddhas of the ten quarters.

'For this reason this Bodhisattva is named the Unlimited Light; it is with this light of wisdom that he shines over all beings and causes them to be removed from the three paths of existence, hells, pretas, and the brute creation, and to obtain the highest power. For the same reason, this Bodhisattva is called the Bodhisattva of Great Strength, Mahasthama. His heavenly crown has five hundred jewel-flowers; each jewel-flower has

five hundred jewel-towers; in each tower are seen manifested all the pure and excellent features of the far-stretching Buddha countries in the ten quarters. The turban on his head is like a padma (lotus) flower; on the top of the turban there is a jewel-pitcher, which is filled with various brilliant rays fully manifesting the state of Buddha. All his other bodily signs are quite equal to those of Avalokitesvara. When this Bodhisattva walks about, all the regions of the ten quarters tremble and quake. Wherever the earth quakes there appear five hundred millions of jewel-flowers; each jewel-flower with its splendid dazzling beauty looks like the World of Highest Happiness, Sukhavati.

'When this Bodhisattva sits down, all the countries of seven jewels at once tremble and quake; all the incarnate Amitayus's, innumerable as the dust of the earth, and all the incarnate Bodhisattvas who dwell in the middlemost Buddha countries situated between the Buddha country of the lower region presided over by a Buddha called the "Golden Light," and the country of the upper region presided over by a Buddha called the "King of Light,"—all these

assemble in the World of Highest Happiness, Sukhavati, like gathering clouds sit on their thrones of lotus flowers, which fill the whole sky, and preach the excellent Law in order to deliver all the beings that are plunged in suffering;—such is the perception of the form and body of Bodhisattva Mahasthama, and it is the **Eleventh Meditation.**

'Those who practise this meditation are freed from the sins which would otherwise involve them in births and deaths for innumerable kalpas.

'Those who have practised this meditation do not live in an embryo state but obtain free access to the excellent and admirable countries of Buddhas. Those who have experienced this are said to have perfectly meditated upon the two Bodhisattvas, Avalokitesvara and Mahasthama.

'After thou hast had this perception, thou shouldst imagine thyself to be born in the World of Highest Happiness in the western quarter, and to be seated, cross-legged, on a lotus flower there. Then imagine that the flower has shut thee in

and has afterwards unfolded; when the flower has thus unfolded, five hundred coloured rays will shine over thy body, thine eyes will be opened so as to see the Buddhas and Bodhisattvas who fill the whole sky; thou wilt hear the sounds of waters and trees, the notes of birds, and the voices of many Buddhas preaching the excellent Law, in accordance with the twelve divisions of the scriptures. When thou hast ceased from that meditation, thou must remember the experience ever after.

'If thou hast passed through this experience thou art said to have seen the World of Highest Happiness in the realm of the Buddha Amitayus; —this is the perception obtained by a complete meditation on that Buddha country, and is called the **Twelfth Meditation**.

'The innumerable incarnate bodies of Amitayus, together with those of Avalokitesvara and Mahasthama, constantly come and appear before such devotees as above mentioned.'

Buddha then spoke to Ananda and Vaidehi: 'Those who wish, by means of their serene

thoughts, to be born in the western land, should first meditate on an image of the Buddha, who is sixteen cubits high, seated on a lotus flower in the water of the lake. As it was stated before, the real body and its measurement are unlimited, incomprehensible to the ordinary mind.

'But by the efficacy of the ancient prayer of that Tathagata, those who think of and remember him shall certainly be able to accomplish their aim.

'Even the mere perceiving of the image of that Buddha brings to one immeasurable blessings. How much more, then, will the meditating upon all the complete bodily signs of that Buddha! Buddha Amitayus has supernatural power; since everything is at his disposal, he freely transforms himself in the regions of the ten quarters. At one time he shows himself as possessing a magnificent body, which fills the whole sky, at another he makes his body appear small, the height being only sixteen or eighteen cubits. The body he manifests is always pure gold in colour; his halo—bright with transformed Buddhas—and his jewel lotus flowers are as mentioned above. The bodies of the two Bodhisattvas are the same always.

'All beings can recognise either of the two Bodhisattvas by simply glancing at the marks of their heads. These two Bodhisattvas assist Amitayus in his work of universal salvation;—such is the meditation that forms a joint perception of the Buddha and Bodhisattvas, and it is the **Thirteenth Meditation.**'

First sermon at Sarnath

3

Buddha then spoke to Ananda and Vaidehi: 'The beings who will be born in the highest form of the highest grade, i.e., to Buddhahood, are those, whoever they may be, who wish to be born in that country and cherish the threefold thought whereby they are at once destined to be born there. What is the threefold thought, you may ask. First, the True Thought; second, the Deep Believing Thought; third, the Desire to be Born in that Pure Land by bringing one's own stock of merit to maturity. Those who have this threefold thought in perfection shall most assuredly be born into that country.

'There are also three classes of beings who are able to be born in that country. What, you may ask, are the three classes of beings? First, those who are possessed of a compassionate mind, who do no injury to any beings, and accomplish all virtuous actions according to Buddha's precepts; second, those who study and recite the sutras of the Mahayana doctrine, for instance, the Vaipulya Sutras; third, those who practise the sixfold remembrance. These three classes of beings who wish to be born in that country by bringing their

respective stocks of merit to maturity, will become destined to be born there if they have accomplished any of those meritorious deeds for one day or even for seven days.

'When one who has practised these merits is about to be born in that country, Buddha Amitayus, together with the two Bodhisattvas also numberless created Buddhas, and a hundred thousand Bhikshus and Sravakas, with their whole retinue, and innumerable gods, together with the palaces of seven jewels, will appear before him out of regard for his diligence and courage; Avalokitesvara, together with Mahasthama will offer a diamond seat to him; thereupon Amitayus himself will send forth magnificent rays of light to shine over the dying person's body. He and many Bodhisattvas will offer their hands and welcome him, when Avalokitesvara Mahasthama and all the other Bodhisattvas will praise the glory of the man who practised the meritorious deeds, and convey an exhortation to his mind.

'When the newcomer, having seen these, rejoicing and leaping for joy, looks at himself, he will find his own body seated on that diamond throne; and as he follows behind Buddha he will be born into that country, in a moment. When

he has been born there, he will see Buddha's form and body with every sign of perfection complete, and also the perfect forms and signs of all the Bodhisattvas; he will also see brilliant rays and jewel-forests and hear them propounding the excellent Law, and instantly be conscious of a spirit of resignation to whatever consequences may hereafter arise.

'Before long he will serve everyone of the Buddhas who live in the regions of the ten quarters. In the presence of each of those Buddhas he will obtain successively a prophecy of his future destiny. On his return to his own land Sukhavati, in which he has just been born he will obtain countless hundreds of thousands of Dharani formulas' mystic form of prayer;—such are those who are to be born in the highest form of the highest grade to Buddhahood.

'Next, the beings who will be born in the middle form of the highest grade are those who do not necessarily learn, remember, study, or recite those Vaipulya Sutras, but fully understand the meaning of the truth contained in them, and having a firm grasp of the highest truth do not

speak evil of the Mahayana doctrine, but deeply believe in the principle of cause and effect; who by bringing these good qualities to maturity seek to be born in that Country of Highest Happiness.

'When one who has acquired these qualities is about to die, Amitayus, surrounded by the two Bodhisattvas Avalokitesvara and Mahasthama and an innumerable retinue of dependents, will bring a seat of purple gold and approach him with words of praise, saying: "O my son in the Law! thou hast practised the Mahayana doctrine; thou hast understood and believed the highest truth; therefore I now come to meet and welcome thee." He and the thousand created Buddhas offer hands all at once.

'When that man looks at his own body, he will find himself seated on that purple gold seat; he will, then, stretching forth his folded hands, praise and eulogise all the Buddhas. As quick as thought he will be born in the lake of seven jewels of that country. That purple gold seat on which he sits is like a magnificent jewel-flower, and will open after a night; the newcomer's body becomes purple gold in colour, and he will also find under his feet a lotus flower consisting of seven jewels.

Buddha and the Bodhisattvas at the same time will send forth brilliant rays to shine over the body of that person whose eyes will instantaneously be opened and become clear. According to his former usage in the human world, he will hear all the voices that are there, preaching primary truths of the deepest significance.

'Then he will descend from that golden seat and worship Buddha with folded hands, praising and eulogising the World-Honoured One. After seven days, he will immediately attain to the state of the highest perfect knowledge (anuttara samyaksambodhi) from which he will never fall away; next he will fly to all the ten regions and successively serve all the Buddhas therein; he will practise many a Samadhi in the presence of those Buddhas. After the lapse of a lesser kalpa he will attain a spirit of resignation to whatever consequences may hereafter arise, and he will also obtain a prophecy of his future destiny in the presence of Buddhas.

'Next are those who are to be born in the lowest form of the highest grade: this class of beings also believes in the principle of cause and

effect, and without slandering the Mahayana doctrine, simply cherishes the thought of obtaining the highest Bodhi and by bringing this good quality to maturity, seeks to be born in that Country of Highest Happiness. When a devotee of this class dies, Amitayus, with Avalokitesvara and Mahasthama and all the dependents, will offer him a golden lotus flower; he will also miraculously create five hundred Buddhas in order to send and meet him.

'These five hundred created Buddhas will, all at once, offer hands and praise him, saying: "O my son in the Law! thou art pure now; as thou hast cherished the thought of obtaining the highest Bodhi, we come to meet thee." When he has seen them, he will find himself seated on that golden lotus flower. Soon the flower wiII close upon him; following behind the World-Honoured One he will go to be born in the lake of seven jewels. After one day and one night the lotus flower will unfold itself. Within seven days he may see the Buddha's body, though his mind is not as yet clear enough to perceive all the signs and marks of the Buddha, which he will be able to see clearly after three weeks; then he will hear many sounds and voices

preaching the excellent Law, and he himself, travelling through all the ten quarters, will worship all the Buddhas, from whom he will learn the deepest significance of the Law. After three lesser kalpas he will gain entrance to the knowledge of a hundred divisions of nature and become settled in the first joyful stage of Bodhisattva. The perception on of these three classes of beings is called the meditation upon the superior class of beings, and is the **Fourteenth Meditation.**

'The beings who will be born in the highest form of the middle grade are those who observe the five prohibitive precepts, the eight prohibitive precepts and the fasting, and practise all the moral precepts; who do not commit the five deadly sins, and who bring no blame or trouble upon any beings; and who by bringing these good qualities to maturity seek to be born in the World of Highest Happiness in the western quarter. On the eve of such a person's departure from this life, Amitayus, surrounded by Bhikshus and dependents, will appear before him, flashing forth rays of golden colour, and will preach the Law of suffering, non-existence, impermanence, and non-

self. He will also praise the virtue of homelessness that can liberate one from all sufferings. At the sight of Buddha, that believer will excessively rejoice in his heart; he will soon find himself seated on a lotus flower. Kneeling down on the ground and stretching forth his folded hands he will pay homage to Buddha. Before he raises his head he will reach that Country of Highest Happiness and be born there. Soon the lotus flower will unfold, when he will hear sounds and voices praising and glorifying the Four Noble Truths of suffering. He will immediately attain to the fruition of Arhatship, gain the threefold knowledge and the six supernatural faculties, and complete the eightfold emancipation.

'The beings who will be born in the middle form of the middle grade are those who either observe the eight prohibitive precepts, and the fasting for one day and one night, or observe the prohibitive precept for Sramanera, a novice for the same period, or observe the perfect moral precepts, not lowering their dignity nor neglecting any ceremonial observance for one day and one night, and by bringing their respective merits to maturity seek to be born in the Country of

Highest Happiness. On the eve of departure from this life, such a believer who is possessed of this moral virtue, which he has made fragrant by cultivation during his life, will see Amitayus, followed by all his retinue; flashing forth rays of golden colour, this Buddha will come before him and offer a lotus flower of seven jewels.

'He will hear a voice in the sky, praising him and saying: "O son of a noble family, thou art indeed an excellent man. Out of regard for thy obedience to the teachings of all the Buddhas of the three worlds I, now, come and meet thee." Then the newcomer will see himself seated on that lotus flower. Soon the lotus flower will fold around him, and being in this he will be born in the jewel-lake of the World of Highest Happiness in the western quarter.

'After seven days that flower will unfold again, when the believer will open his eyes, and praise the World-Honoured One, stretching forth his folded hands. Having heard the Law, he will rejoice and obtain the fruition of a Srotapanna, the first grade to Nirvana.

'In the lapse of half a kalpa he will become an Arhat.

'Next are the beings who will be born in the lowest form of the middle grade to Buddhahood. If there be sons or daughters of a noble family who are filial to their parents and support them, besides exercising benevolence and compassion in the world, at their departure from this life, such persons will meet a good and learned teacher who will fully describe to them the state of happiness in that Buddha country of Amitayus, and will also explain the forty-eight prayers of the Bhikshu Dharmakara. As soon as any such person has heard these details, his life will come to an end. In a brief moment he will be born in the World of Highest Happiness in the western quarter.

'After seven days he will meet Avalokitesvara and Mahasthama from whom he will learn the Law and rejoice. After the lapse of a lesser kalpa he will attain to the fruition of an Arhat. The perception of these three sorts of beings is called the meditation of the middle class of beings, and is the **Fifteenth Meditation**.

'Next are the beings who will be born in the highest form of the lowest grade. If there be anyone who commits many evil deeds, provided that he does not speak evil of the Mahavaipulya Sutras,

he, though himself a very stupid man, and neither ashamed nor sorry for all the evil actions that he has done, yet, while dying, may meet a good and learned teacher who will recite and laud the headings and titles of the twelve divisions of the Mahayana scriptures. Having thus heard the names of all the Sutras, he will be freed from the greatest sins which would involve him in births and deaths during a thousand kalpas.

'A wise man also will teach him to stretch forth his folded hands and to say, "Adoration to Buddha Amitayus" (Namo-mitabhaya Buddhaya, or, Namo-miuyushe Buddhaya). Having uttered the name of the Buddha, he will be freed from the sins which would otherwise involve him in births and deaths for fifty millions of kalpas. Thereupon the Buddha will send a created Buddha, and the created Bodhisattvas Avalokitesvara and Mahasthama to approach that person with words of praise, saying: "O son of a noble family, as thou hast uttered the name of that Buddha, all thy sins have been destroyed and expiated, and therefore we now come to meet thee." After this speech the devotee will observe the rays of that created Buddha flooding his chamber with light, and while rejoicing at the sight he will depart this life. Seated on a lotus flower he

will follow that created Buddha and go to be born in the jewel-lake.

'After the lapse of seven weeks, the lotus flower will unfold, when the great compassionate Bodhisattvas Avalokitesavara and Mahasthama will stand before him, flashing forth magnificent rays, and will preach to him the deepest meaning of the twelve divisions of the scriptures. Having heard this, he will understand and believe it, and cherish the thought of attaining the highest Bodhi. In a period of ten lesser kalpas he will gain entrance to the knowledge of the hundred divisions of nature, and be able to enter upon the first joyful stage of Bodhisattva. Those who have, had an opportunity of hearing the name of Buddha, the name of the Law, and the name of the Church—the names of the Three Jewels—can also be born in that country.'

Buddha continued: 'Next are the beings who will be born in the middle form of the lowest grade. If there be anyone who transgresses the five and the eight prohibitive precepts, and also all the perfect moral precepts; he, being himself so stupid as to steal things that belong to the whole community, or things that belong to a particular Bhikshu, and not be ashamed nor sorry for his

impure preaching of the Law, but magnify and glorify himself with many wicked deeds:—such a sinful person deserves to fall into hell in consequence of those sins. At the time of his death, when the fires of hell approach him from all sides, he will meet a good and learned teacher who will, out of great compassion, preach the power and virtue of the ten faculties of Amitayus and fully explain the supernatural powers and brilliant rays of that Buddha; and will further praise moral virtue, meditation, wisdom, emancipation, and the thorough knowledge that follows emancipation.

'After having heard this, he will be freed from his sins, which would involve him in births and deaths during eighty millions of kalpas; thereupon those violent fires of hell will transform themselves into a pure and cool wind blowing about heavenly flowers. On each of these flowers will stand a created Buddha or Bodhisattva to meet and receive that person. In a moment he will be born in a lotus flower growing in the lake of seven jewels. After six kalpas the lotus flower will open, when Avalokitesvara and Mahasthama will soothe and encourage him with their Brahma-voices, and preach to him the Mahayana Sutras of the deepest significance.

Arriving !

'Having heard this Law, he will instantaneously direct his thought toward the attainment of the highest Bodhi.

'Lastly, the beings who will be born in the lowest form of the lowest grade. If there be anyone who commits evil deeds, and even completes the ten wicked actions, the five deadly sins and the like; that man, being himself stupid and guilty of many crimes, deserves to fall into a miserable path of existence and suffer endless pains during many kalpas. On the eve of his death he will meet a good and learned teacher who will, soothing and encouraging him in various ways, preach to him the excellent Law and teach him the remembrance of Buddha, but, being harassed by pains, he will have no time to think of Buddha.

'Some good friend will then say to him: "Even if thou canst not exercise the remembrance of Buddha, thou mayst, at least, utter the name, Buddha Amitayus." Let him do so serenely with his voice uninterrupted; let him be continually thinking of Buddha until he has completed ten times the thought, repeating the formula, "Adoration to Buddha Amitayus" (Namomitayushe Buddhaya). On the strength of his merit of uttering Buddha's name he will, during

every repetition, expiate the sins which involve him in births and deaths during eighty millions of kalpas. He will, while dying, see a golden lotus flower like the disk of the sun appearing before his eyes; in a moment he will be born in the World of Highest Happiness. After twelve greater kalpas the lotus flower will unfold; thereupon the Bodhisattvas Avalokitesvara and Mahasthama, raising their voices in great compassion, will preach to him in detail the real state of all the elements of nature and the law of the expiation of sins.

'On hearing them he will rejoice and will immediately direct his thought toward the attainment of the Bodhi;—such are the beings who are to be born in the lowest form of the lowest grade to Buddhahood. The perception of the above three is called the meditation of the inferior class of beings, and is the **Sixteenth Meditation**.'

4

When Buddha had finished this speech, Vaidehi, together with her five hundred female attendants, could see, as guided by the Buddha's words, the scene of the far-stretching World of the Highest Happiness, and could also see the body of Buddha and the bodies of the two Bodhisattvas. With her mind filled with joy she praised them, saying: 'Never have I seen such a wonder!' Instantaneously she became wholly and fully enlightened, and attained a spirit of resignation, prepared to endure whatever consequences might yet arise. Her five hundred female attendants too cherished the thought of obtaining the highest perfect knowledge, and sought to be born in that Buddha country.

The World-Honoured One predicted that they would all be born in that Buddha country, and be able to obtain the Samadhi the supernatural calm of the presence of many Buddhas. All the innumerable Devas also directed their thought toward the attainment of the highest Bodhi.

Thereupon Ananda rose from his seat, approached Buddha, and spoke thus: 'O World-

Honoured One, what should we call this Sutra? And how should we receive and remember it in the future? '

Buddha said in his reply to Ananda: 'O Ananda, this Sutra should be called the meditation on the Land of Sukhavati, on Buddha Amitayus, Bodhisattva Avalokitesvara, Bodhisattva Mahasthama, or otherwise be called "the Sutra on the entire removal of the obstacle of Karma, the means of being born in the realm of the Buddhas." Thou shouldst take and hold it, not forgetting nor losing it. Those who practise the Samadhi in accordance with this Sutra will be able to see, in the present life, Buddha Amitayus and the two great Bodhisattvas.

'In case of a son or a daughter of a noble family, the mere hearing of the names of the Buddha and the two Bodhisattvas will expiate the sins which would involve them in births and deaths during innumerable kalpas. How much more will the remembrance of Buddha and the Bodhisattvas!

'Know that he who remembers that Buddha is the white lotus among men, it is he whom the

Bodhisattvas Avalokitesvara and Mahasthama consider an excellent friend. He will, sitting in the Bodhi-mandala, be born in the abode of Buddhas.'

Buddha further spoke to Ananda: 'Thou shouldst carefully remember these words. To remember these words is to remember the name of Buddha Amitayus.'

When Buddha concluded these words, the worthy disciples Mahamaudgalyayana, and Ananda, Vaidehi, and the others were all enraptured with excessive joy.

Thereupon the World-Honoured One came back, walking through the open sky, to the Mount Gridhrakuta. Ananda soon after spoke before a great assembly, of all the occurrences as stated above. On hearing this, all the innumerable Devas, Nagas, and Yakshas were inspired with great joy; and having worshipped the Buddha they went their way.

Here ends the Sutra of the Meditation on Buddha Amitayus, spoken by Buddha Sakyamuni.

• • •

Other Titles are Available in

PHILOSOPHY, RELIGION & CULTURE